To Ann

THE PA & EA CIRCUS

Integrating the many parts of the
Personal and Executive Assistant

Many congrats!!

*Angela
Garry
x*

ANGELA GARRY

The world's most connected
Personal Assistant and PA Trainer

First published by PICA BOOKS (www.picabooks.co.uk)

via the printing services of CreateSpace.com

British Library Cataloguing-in-Publication Data

A catalogue entry for this book is available

from the British Library.

ISBN-13: 978-1505682366 ISBN-10:1505682363

Printed and bound in the UK by CreateSpace.com

DEDICATION

To the people
who make it all worthwhile:
I love you all.

Onwards and upwards!!

OTHER PUBLICATIONS BY ANGELA GARRY

<u>For Personal Assistants, Executive Assistants, Secretaries and Administrators:</u>

"Brave PAs – the ultimate guide to being outstanding in a tough job" – for staff working in education.
Published: March 2015, by Independent Thinking Press, an imprint of Crown House Publishing Ltd (www.crownhouse.co.uk)
Review by Executive PA magazine: "the new PA Bible" (April 2015).

"NAHPA" – National Association of Headteachers' PAs magazine.
Published three times per year, once per school term, by Pica Aurum (www.nahpa.org.uk)
The UK & Ireland's leading publication for PAs and Administrative Staff in Education.

<u>Therapeutic fiction for children and young adults (written and designed to be both read alone, and with families, carers, support workers, teachers):</u>

"Missing Mark: understanding loss"
A therapeutic story book for children and young adults.
Published: June 2015, by PICA BOOKS (www.picabooks.co.uk)

"Darcy Decides: coping with family breakups and changes"
A therapeutic story book for children and young adults.
Published: August 2015, by PICA BOOKS (www.picabooks.co.uk)

ACKNOWLEDGMENTS

I'd like to acknowledge all the PAs, EAs, VAs, Secretaries and Administrative Staff with whom I've worked in my own career as a PA / Admin in corporate and industry environments, for demonstrating their professionalism and determination to be the best they can be in their roles – and for encouraging me to grow in mine.

I'd also like to acknowledge all those I've met on my networking, coaching, mentoring and training jaunts in the UK and around the world – it would be nigh on impossible to successfully do my work without their generosity in sharing their expertise, experiences and enthusiasm for their careers.

To both of these groups – you are all incredibly talented and brilliant – and I wish you all the success in the world.

Thanks also must go to Debra Jarrett for assisting with editing and proofing, and Lucy Brazier for contributing the book's Foreword.

CONTENTS

FOREWORD
BY LUCY BRAZIER

Back in 2011 when we relaunched 'Executive Secretary' magazine, one of the first profiles that we featured was that of Angela Garry – the most connected Assistant on the planet. Back then, Angela was working as the Principal's Personal Assistant in an inner city secondary school, but had somehow managed to build a network of LinkedIn contacts greater than any other Assistant in the world.

From the off, it was clear that Angela's aim was similar to our own; to ensure that Assistants were recognised for the incredible work that they do. In the five years that have passed since we first featured her, she has made a new career for herself as one of the world's most recognisable faces in the training arena for Assistants – particularly in her own field of education and as an advocate for the profession. And make no mistake – it is no longer just a job. It is a profession.

There is no doubt that since the recession, seven years ago, that the Assistant's world has taken on the appearance of a circus. With middle management being made redundant and Assistants being asked to step up and take on those roles, usually resulting in workloads increasing by upwards of 25% and the majority of Assistants also finding themselves with an ever increasing number of Executives, the role has changed beyond recognition. Last year, the ASAP, one of the USA's largest associations, proved categorically that Assistants are the new middle management. And yet the perception within the businesses that they serve and the remuneration attached so often hasn't caught up.

Our latest research conducted in association with Avery shows that an Assistants' IQ (intelligence quotient) is as high as their peers' in the office but their EQ (emotional intelligence quotient) is off the top of the scale. They are prepared to take on projects and tasks with no training, yet somehow make it work. And they work considerably more overtime than most other members of staff. In many ways they are the ideal employee.

This, combined with recent research conducted by Hays, raises questions of both Assistants themselves and the businesses that they serve that need to be answered. The Hays research shows a huge perception gap in how the Assistants see themselves, and the way that senior management see them. One in ten CEOs see Assistants as equal to their senior management team and over a half as management level, and yet the Assistants don't see themselves like this at all. Maybe this is because most businesses are not investing in Assistant training and salaries in the same way that they are with other members of staff.

With the role changing as it is, the smartest businesses are investing in their Assistants' training and that investment is dropping straight to the bottom line in terms of real savings made to the Executives' time.

Angela Garry's book looks at a role that is at a point of crucial change. Bonnie Low Kramen is fond of saying that there has never been a more exciting time to be an Assistant because everything is changing so fast. I would add that there has never been a scarier time to be an Assistant, because everything is changing so fast! Angela seeks to take away that fear and to make sense of it all.

The Assistant's time is now.

Lucy Brazier

CEO & Founder Marcham Publishing

Publishers of Executive Secretary Magazine

INTRODUCTION

Sometimes I think we are a breed known only to ourselves: Personal Assistants, Executive Assistants, Secretaries, Administrators – whatever you call us, we are all one breed, one species, set apart from the rest of mankind.

We are a magical breed.

We are capable of magical things. We find ways to make the impossible task possible, we conjure things out of thin air, we find a way to make whatever it is work. We anticipate the needs of our boss before the boss recognises that they need them.

We organise and create, often on almost no budget at all, the most stunning events and happenings. We have contact lists that would be the envy of every salesman in the land who wishes to market a product into an organisation.

We are the unicorns of the office.

We do things that others will not, cannot, or do not want to do, many of which they have no idea *how* to do. We have ways of making things happen, we know who is the right person to get in touch with about almost any situation, we are calm and unflappable in the worst of circumstances. We might not know the answer, but we will find out.

We keep the organisation going in the absence of the boss, we work hard to keep the 'un-wanteds' away from the boss, we protect the boss's time. We fulfil a multitude of roles and responsibilities, and we get the job done – pretty much regardless of whatever it is.

We multi-task and wear a multitude of 'hats' to enable us to carry out our varying responsibilities.

We are the ringleader and almost every other role at the circus.

A great PA is made up of a large number of different parts – effectively taking on all of the different roles involved in a circus – which we need to nurture and carefully integrate into a cohesive whole in order to put on the greatest show on earth: supporting our Executives in running the organisation.

This book is based on my own experiences of over 24 years working in administration, plus it includes insights from some of the amazing PAs / EAs around the world whom I've had the tremendous good fortune to meet in recent years. It has been an honour to work with, train and mentor them, and to experience their generosity and openness in sharing with me their own career highlights and lowlights: their frustrations, their proudest moments, their laughter and, in a couple of cases, a few tears.

Just think: in what other profession might someone find themselves in these sort of situations?

- On a day trip from New York to Niagara Falls: one EA told me she ended up helping the disorganised tour guide organise the tickets, rounding up the tour group at Buffalo airport and making name badges for everyone on the trip. All whilst on holiday.... just doing what came naturally!
- Shopping in Dublin: advising a sign painter outside a shop on changing the wording he'd just painted, as it wasn't grammatically correct and contained two spelling mistakes. A PA in Ireland related to me that she just couldn't bear to walk past without attempting to fix things, having seen such glaring errors.
- On a train to London: when I was working full-time and editing a magazine in my fictitious "spare time", I created a sample layout for a magazine and edited several articles for it, armed only with an iPhone. This was on the way home from a 12-hour conference and dinner... I could have slept, but the deadline was coming up and I wanted to include a write-up on the conference in an article.
- In the car in a traffic jam: instead of stressing over the traffic, many PAs and EAs make good use of their time by listening to language CDs and mp3s in order to become fluent in another language which is used within offices of their organisation elsewhere in the world.
- Somewhere over the Arab Emirates: chatting with a fellow traveller on a flight then looking them up on the internet afterwards in order to keep in touch. The PA in question told me that all she had to go on was the other traveller's first name and a TV show she worked on in Poland: an easy task for a serial Googler!!

Today's PAs and EAs do all of these and more. In fact, these are just some of the ways we have embraced new technologies to help us make the most of us time with least effort – to follow the adage of not working harder, but working SMARTER. (We'll look at this in detail later in the book.)

We take on so many roles within our businesses – each chapter in the book relates to some different aspect or part of ourselves through which we perform an aspect of our work. "The PA & EA Circus" looks at those parts individually – and how we can integrate them to become the best possible PA or EA that we can be. It should be noted that there are actually far more roles that we undertake than there are chapters: this book doesn't touch on the work of Financial PAs, for example, or Legal Secretaries, Medical Secretaries, etc. With around 160 job titles worldwide for what we do, this could turn into being an encyclopaedia if I were to attempt to cover ALL of the various parts, so I had to decide to draw a line as to how many parts to look at!

The roles of PA and EA have evolved steadily over the years and are now far more than the secretarial position from which they originated. However, perceptions of the roles haven't progressed at the same rate, with many people still believing them to be rooted in basic administration. In order to redefine the role, PAs and EAs need to give themselves and their roles the respect they deserve. The truly excellent PA or EA is at the heart of the business and, as well as being heavily relied upon, is highly influential at a very senior level. Very few of your colleagues are in daily contact with the managing director of their company – but you are. Do not underestimate your importance.

One immediate thing I can recommend to you, before reading any further, is that you should be sharing knowledge and networking with your peers. There is a wealth of information out there in the minds of other PAs and EAs – and with the internet so easily accessible to us why on earth should anyone waste time and effort in finding out solutions to problems that others have already experienced? Share you knowledge, learn from others, build the PA and EA community – show the world that we are a force to be reckoned with!

LinkedIn is superb source for networking and creating some great business contacts – plus the discussion groups make it easy to communicate with others. Not only can you find valuable help and advice for you in your role, but you can also make someone else's role a lot easier by sharing your expertise.

My other introductory words of advice are a little difficult to put into practice sometimes , but I am sure they will resonate with many of you: "Selectively say 'yes', but more importantly learn to say 'no' to your colleagues and executives". Don't take on every task and project just because you are the resident 'expert' – push some of the work back at an appropriate level, and delegate more to others. It can feel hard to decline a request, but saying no is a skill we all need to practise at times. A route to this is found in a quote from inspirational speaker Brené Brown Ph.D., who advises us to "choose discomfort over resentment". She advocates that the discomfort of saying 'no' is preferable to the resentment we feel by saying 'yes' to taking on a task that we don't have time to.

Saving time is a major theme throughout "The PA Circus". If by reading this book, you find some information, hint, tip, idea or technique which could save you just an hour per week at work, just think what you are going to be able to achieve in those additional 50+ hours (a free working week!!) that you'll save over the course of a year – whilst running the circus of your business all the while.

Welcome to The PA & EA Circus!

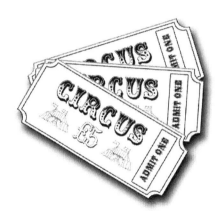

A few notes before we start:

I have changed names in order to 'protect the innocent / not-so-innocent' if necessary in some anecdotes – but all of them at true representations of actual events. Where I have people's permission, names are included to in order give credit where it is due.

This book is intended for anyone working in an administrative role who wants to further their career – whether you are in the lowest level of administrative in your organisation or the highest.

Notes on job titles:

"The PA Circus" is the Corporate & Industry follow-up to my first book "Brave PAs" for those working in Education. As with "Brave PAs", to save on any confusion whilst you are reading, I am aware that there are around 160 different job titles adopted by administrative staff worldwide – but it would take forever to list them all whenever I mention any roles. Please forgive me, therefore if I don't specifically name your title. For brevity, I'm going with "PA" and "EA" throughout this book – to cover PA, EA, VA, Secretary, Administrator, and all the others. Equally, rather than refer to your boss as "Chairman, Chief Executive, Managing Director, Director or otherwise", I use "Executive" and "boss" pretty much throughout this book.

Notes on gender:

Administrative roles started out in early history as a male occupation. From the ancient scribes and monks who wrote down and passed on information to the next generation, to the "aide de camp" assistants in the military and political fields who acted as advisors to leading soldiers, politicians and royalty – these roles were all carried out by men. The Pitman secretarial school was founded by Sir Isaac Pitman in 1870 for "professional and commercial men". The situation changed and women started entering the administrative world after the typewriter was invented in the late 1890s and the subsequent World War when the men went to war and women went to replace them in the workplace. It has since been noted that:

a) women were cheaper than men as we would accept lower wages without question (on average, women in the UK are paid 16% less than men in the same roles, plus taking time out for raising children women have lower progression rates typically within their roles), and

b) women are natural multi-taskers – there is scientific evidence that the female brain is more adept at managing multiple tasks, seemingly making women 'better suited' for administrative roles than men.

Figures – within the UK at least – back this up: according to a survey by the Association of Personal Assistants in 2012 with 21,000 respondents, 97% of

PAs in the UK are women. In my 24 years of working in administration, I've met less than 10 male Personal Assistants overall.

In addition, other recent studies show that women only make up approximately 18% of board directors in the UK, much lower than the 'leading figure' of 31% in China.

It might seem, therefore, that this book is just for women who work for men. NOT SO!

> **This book is for ALL administrative workers, male or female, in PA / EA / VA / secretary / administrative roles, whether you work for a male or female boss.**

As long as you are interested in furthering your career…

As long as you have an active interest in being the best you can be at whatever it is you do in your role…

And as long as I have breathe left in my body with which to enthuse to you about your importance in your organisation and to motivate you about the dizzying heights that you and your career can get to…

Then:

YOU are my target audience for this book.

WELCOME TO THE GREATEST SHOW ON EARTH:

THE PA & EA CIRCUS!

1. THE CIRCUS RINGLEADER – THE PA / EA

*Every circus needs a **Ringleader** to ensure that the show runs smoothly*

Supporting the Chief Executive, Chairman, Managing Director, or other leadership members, the PA / EA is usually in a unique position in an organisation. We know what's going on, where, who's involved, who's "in the know", and when it is due to be done by. We get to know each department or directorate, and what each is doing in relation to the others. We support our Executive and carry out tasks in their absence, making certain decisions on their behalf. By working closely with them, we internalise much of their skills and knowledge, which we need if we are to be able to answer their calls and correspondence in a confident and professionally knowledgeable manner.

But before we start looking deeper into the various aspects of our work, let's start with a quick check to make sure we are all on the same page on just who and what we are talking about when I write "PA" or "EA" in this book. We'll start with a few questions in an attempt to clarify what can be a muddy area…

What is a PA and an EA – or an EPA, for that matter?

What's the difference between a PA and an EA – and between either of them and a secretary or an admin assistant?

And what is a VA?

What levels of experience, expertise and knowledge are required for each? And what do the letters even stand for?

If you are anything like me, YDDWWA (you don't do well with acronyms).

So here is a quick glossary of the major ones that will be used in this book:

PA   **Personal Assistant**

EA   **Executive Assistant**

EPA   **Executive Personal Assistant**

VA   **Virtual Assistant** (working from home or elsewhere, often for several companies)

Effectively – the PA / EA / EPA role is the leading support role in an organisation, supporting the leader(s) of the company: the Chief Executive, the Chairman, the Directors.

But didn't Secretaries used to do that, supporting the leader?

What's the difference between a PA or an EA and a secretary?

And which role is higher than the other?

Hmmm. Here, we enter into quite a bit of confusion over what the roles actually entail – and public perception of them. There can be a lot of confusion between levels and rankings– particularly from one industry or type of organisation to another. There are around 160 job titles within senior administration which fulfil many of the roles of the PA / EA / EPA / VA including Secretary, Senior Secretary, Administrative Assistant, Administrator, Office Manager.

Subsequently, it can be very difficult to work out the hierarchy and levels of responsibility within a group of administrative roles, as the names of roles are not always the same (nor do they carry the same weight) from one industry to another. For example: the role of Secretary of State in the USA is fourth in line to the Presidency – a secretary of the very highest level.

Another example is shown in my own employment history: my first two roles (and their titles) after I graduated from University.

- In my first job, I worked at a utility company (in the ultra-glamorous world of Water and Sewerage, no less!) – where my role was Administrative Assistant. I was the lowest level administrative staff member in the department, the next person up from me was the Administrator for the department (Helen), and my line manager was Suzanne, the Secretary to one of the company's Directors.
- I then temped for a few months before moving to my second major role – which changed my idea of administrative hierarchy completely... I moved to a job in the School of Education of a University where I was a Senior Secretary working for a group of Academics. My line manager was Betsy, the Administrative Assistant who was the second highest administrative staff member in the School – and she in turn was line managed by the Administrator, Peter.

This meant that in one of these roles, the Administrative Assistant was the lowest role – yet in the other, the post-holder was the second in command... This can be confusing and to people outside the environment, perceptions can be muddied about the differences between one role and another.

Traditionally, the role of the Secretary has been one that fulfils the tasks given to them – taking dictation and producing letters, for example. In most organisations the role remained at this level of responsibility. This, in particular, is the role we most often see depicted in the media (films, television, books): a 1950s style "Take a letter, Miss Jones". There will be a little more on that later.

In more recent years, with the advent of smaller and more advanced technology and our managers having an ever-increasing workload, they have needed us to take on more responsibility, more accountability, has more input into the work they are doing, and is trusted to make more decisions on behalf of their Executive.

The role of the PA / EA has developed to fill this gap, usually bearing much more responsibility and autonomy than the secretary role of old.

From my experiences of meeting PAs and EAs worldwide during my training work, it seems that the title given at the top level in most organisations is more likely to be 'Personal Assistant' within the United Kingdom, whereas in some other countries like the United States the role is more often titled 'Executive Assistant'. And of course there are exceptions to this – some organisations have both, with the Executive Assistant's role, responsibilities and influence being higher than those of the Personal Assistant.

In addition to these roles, there are also then Assistant roles working for private individuals or households, including celebrities and royalty – who very often take on many much more personalised tasks for their 'boss', looking after their household and issues in their personal lives as well as handling their business needs.

"COMING SOON:
THE CIRCUS IS COMING SOON!

2. WHAT SKILLS DO YOU NEED TO RUN THE SHOW?

The circus arrives in town: but before we can get the show into full swing, what skills do you need to run the show?

If you are brand new to being a PA or EA, then welcome to this really exciting profession!

Being a new PA / EA is no easy task. Your Executive will quite often expect things of you that you are unfamiliar with – they may presume that you already know what to do without being told.

They will probably also expect that you automatically know their preferences and be able to organise logistics successfully on their behalf.

If you want to be great at your job, the following pointers should be useful to you.

Be friendly and earn the respect of your colleagues

When you arrive in a new role, your colleagues need to know who you are and what you do – and you need to make sure that they know that when you need something from them you need them to respond accordingly, as you are working on behalf of your Executive.

A major element of the PA role is chasing people to get them to produce reports and papers to deadline, to agree to attend meetings and to turn up on time and to take on extra responsibility, so you need your colleagues to know that you are there as the Executive's 'second voice' and their 'third arm'. You are there to ensure that whatever needs doing for your Executive gets done.

You will need to get to know about the people your boss will meet with on a regular basis – this might include, for example, the organisation's Board of Directors. If they are familiar with who you are and what your role is, a good working relationship with them should develop much easier than if they have no idea who you are or what you are doing. You may not be directly involved with their schedule or time management, but getting acquainted with their assistants will help assure their co-operation when you need something from them.

Start to inform your colleagues about what a PA does…

You will find that, like the majority of the remainder of the world, many of the people you work with have little idea of the role of a PA so your task should be to educate them! Some people may think of you as a diary-keeper, others a chaser-of-deadlines and others still the 'go to' person for everything under the sun, so they will often come to you with questions or tasks that aren't your responsibility to fulfil, but as they have no idea who else to go to with them, they come to you. Of course, these are things that you will take in your stride in time – it usually is the case that "if you don't know who to ask about something, ask the PA / EA – they will be able to find out for you".

For example, many of your colleagues will be under the impression that you are (apparently) the only person in the entire world who knows where anything is. Without you, nobody would know who to call, when the meeting is or who it is with – and the list keeps going.

Being a PA / EA requires certain skills including organising meetings, handling travel itineraries, having good (or preferably great) computing skills and typing speeds, as well as being flexible and adaptable for working with last minute changes.

In fact, our role requires a range of skills, including organising meetings, handling travel itineraries, having good (or preferably great) computing skills and typing speeds, as well as being flexible and adaptable for working with last minute changes. But, because of their lack of knowledge about the role, a lot of people may assume that the role of PA is easy, which is rather hilarious. I have never met (nor heard of) a PA who has described their job as 'easy'. 'Challenging', 'incredibly worthwhile', 'always varied' – yes – but never 'easy'.

Your role at this point is to enlighten your colleagues. Become an ambassador for the profession and demonstrate to them the true power of the PA – that we essentially control the Executive's time. We decide if and when someone may see our boss or speak to them by phone. We keep the Executive or manager supported in a safety net that allows them to walk the tightrope of running the organisation, whilst secure in the knowledge that we've 'got their back'.

Here are some of the key skills that you will need to develop in order to succeed as a new PA. These are skills that will develop within you over time…

You need to be an elephant

You know the saying, 'Elephants never forget'? PAs must not forget anything because "there's nobody around to back you up".

People *will* come to you looking for a piece of paper they had in their hand six weeks ago or for the contact details of someone who visited the company last year, and even if you had nothing to do with the original details you will be expected to find out.

Your Executive or manager will ask you to 'dig out' an email they received from John or Bob, (or was it Phil?), three or four weeks ago, which mentioned something about X or Y. Undoubtedly, it will turn out to have been a message from Simon, which mentioned that Tim might be involved in a project (to which the Executive had thought, 'No, that's Bob's responsibility'), but you will have to work this out by remembering the conversation you had with the Executive that day when he mentioned something about Bob…

To become great PAs and EAs, we need to develop an almost ESP-type connection with our bosses to work out what it is they mean, because quite often they do not tell us or give us the wrong information.

Great detective skills also help, to piece together the fragments of information that we gather every day…

You need to know everything about everyone

It will also be expected that you know everyone's needs, wants, quirks, habits, demands and eccentricities, because you will, of course, have developed an encyclopaedic knowledge of the staff within the first few moments of having arrived in your new role!

You need to manage time carefully and wisely

There are many different aspects to the role of PA / EA, but one of the most important is that of managing time. And by that I mean both yours AND the person you work for.

You will need to be quick and accurate in the work that you do, adaptable to be able to pick up different tasks at different times and fastidious enough to make sure that nothing gets left behind. You will undoubtedly have a task list a mile long, and it can be quite daunting to a new PA / EA to be suddenly expected to manage this.

You need to manage your manager

By this, I mean that you need to be able to manager your boss's time, their calls and correspondence, their needs and their expectations. You need to make sure that your Executive has time to meet with people, speak with them on the phone and do all of the necessary things that are involved in running a busy organisation.

This means that you will need your calendar synced with theirs, as you will be responsible for ensuring that they get to those meetings at the right time, with the right papers, with the right travel arrangements and knows who they are meeting and why. Your IT team will be able to set it up so that your calendars can work together.

As well as ensuring that your Executive gets to the right meetings, you will be involved in making sure that those meetings happen without a hitch, requiring attention to details such as everyone's availability, preparing papers for the meeting and making sure that everything from the conception of the meeting up to the moment it ends goes smoothly.

Once you've got a handle on their calendar, you will probably also need some sort of access to your Executive's emails too, but very early on in your role, particularly for a new PA / EA, this may not be a requirement just yet. One of the major challenges of the role is to shine

You need to be a great meetings and events organiser

As a PA or EA, you will be the person to organise the next conference or major meetings. Whilst it is highly possible that you enjoy event planning and organising (I do hope so!), nobody around you will have any idea how hard it actually is to organise a full conference. All those who do have an inkling will usually steer clear and leave it to you, as you are the 'trained professional'. This being the case, try to get your name down for a course on event management to help you along.

You need to be the best travel organiser

As well as organising meetings you will quite often be the travel arranger. Anyone who has booked a business trip for six people, all flying from different airports at different times, and all having different personal preferences about the type of place where they want to stay, will be able to tell you that booking travel can be unbelievably complicated – and you will be expected to be the person who can magically make it all happen.

You need to welcome visitors and callers a cheerful and confident air – but block the 'un-wanteds'

In the words of REM, PAs are always 'shiny happy people'. Or at least, we're not supposed to answer the phone or greet visitors at the door with, 'What do you want?' Always aim to shine and be happy to meet the people who come into your room, who call you on the phone, who pass you in the corridor, or outside visitors who come into your organisation. We are there to welcome people into the organisation, and to give them a positive impression of what the organisation does.

However, on the flipside, we need to be able to spot a cold-caller or marketer at 20 paces and, if need be, send them elsewhere or get rid of them politely and firmly. More on this later.

Remember that a key element in being a great PA / EA is enjoying your work. It is not a role that everyone is suited to, because of the enormous amount of multi-tasking required, but it can be incredibly rewarding.

No matter what happens, we will either fix it, sort it out or will know how or who to get it done. Whatever you find yourself doing, use your role to enlighten others and be a great ambassador for the PA and EA profession.

Welcome to the role of PA and EA at your company's circus – get your glad rags on and step out on to the high-wire, it's going to be an exciting time!

"WHO'S GOT THE TENT PEGS AND A MALLET? IS ANYONE GOOD AT PUTTING TENTS UP?"!

3. SETTING UP IN A NEW ROLE

Setting up the Big Top: finding the lay of the land and getting started in a new role

Here are some pointers towards some of the first things you will need to do in the very early days of your new role:

Find, read and digest the handover notes from your predecessor.

What do you mean, there aren't any handover notes?

Check the shelves and drawers in your new office – is there a purple coloured folder anywhere?

(A note for your future self: whenever you leave a job, leave behind some excellent handover notes for your successor – see the "curtain call" chapter towards the end of this book.)

All too often we start at a new job and have to think on our feet on the first day because the person who left the job didn't leave any notes behind. If you find that this is the case when you start a job, make sure that you DO NOT do this to your successor whenever you leave!

OK, so you've read the handover notes (or not, as the case may be).

What's next?

Get set up and find out the basics in your surroundings

- Get set up for computer access. You will need a username and password, access to the network and someone to tell you what's where within the system.

- Telephone access. Do you need a pin number to sign in to the voicemail system? How do you set up speed dials on your desk phone? What is already set up on it? With luck, this should be detailed in the handover notes you receive.

- Access to the boss's email/calendar via the computer network. Some managers will want you to have 'viewing' access only while you and they build up trust; others will expect and need you to have full 'editing' access straightaway.

- Fire and emergency evacuation procedures – where should you go, and what should you do, in the event of an alarm going off?

- Where are the toilets / the canteen / break area? If you are a smoker, where is the smoking area?

- What is the routine for lunches – how do you pay? How often? What time? Where do you go, etc.?

- Is there a safe place for your personal belongings during the day (e.g. do you need a locker or is there a lockable drawer in your desk – with keys)?

- Where are the tea and coffee supplies / printing supplies / stationery cupboard? If you are to order these yourself for your office, who are the suppliers currently used – including contact details?

- Where are the keys to the various filing cabinets and cupboards in your workspace or office?

- Do you need keys to door of your office and/or a security card to 'swipe' your way into the building? And do you need an accompanying identity card?

Get comfortable

Set about rearranging your room and setting up your desk how you want it, including hunting out a more comfortable chair, if necessary, as you are likely to be sitting at your desk for some very long hours at times!

Move things around until you are comfortable with them. (For example, I'm used to working with two screens, with a laptop in front of me and a second monitor and my desk phone to the right, plus a full-size keyboard and mouse in front of the laptop. Trying to work at a desk where the computer and phone are on the wrong side of the desk means I can't work at my best capacity, as I get neck strain from leaning to the left. I have worked with a number of people who have spent years working in uncomfortable positions like this, without resolving the issue by simply moving things around.)

Where is the main source of natural light/electronic light in your office? Do you need to move the actual location of your desk in the room so that you are not blinded by sunlight for certain parts of the day? I've worked with PAs who sit squinting all afternoon in the autumn – when the sun starts to set at just the wrong angle for them to be comfortable – and quite often they haven't moved their desk to alleviate this, saying it would be too troublesome to do. However, squinting in the wrong lighting and getting headaches isn't worth it – so get the desk moved or find out about getting blinds for the window!

Install useful stuff

You may have used various computing aids or shortcuts in previous jobs, such as autocorrects, short words and dictionaries. Now is the time to put them in place in your new role. Also add commonly used work-related website addresses to your browser's favourites list – and if you have done your homework in your last job, you will have created copies of all of these to bring with you before you left. (For more on this, see later.)

Check what computing packages are available to you on your new computer – for example, you may be a whizz with Microsoft Project and used it on a regular basis in your old job, but may find that it is not installed on your computer in your new job. If you anticipate that you are going to need it (and let's face it, you probably will) then you will need to get on to your IT team to see if it can be installed. If the software is already available within the organisation then this should not be a problem, but if it has to be purchased you may need to justify the purchase to your Executive or finance team, as well as the IT team. If you use a digital pen you will need the software for this to be installed on your computer.

Compile your new job's vital statistics

If the following information has not been not provided, then find out your boss's car make / model / registration number, their mobile number, home phone number, their partner's mobile number, name / phone number of their children's schools, contact numbers for their doctor / dentist / parents, the garage for their car and so on.

You will also need the desk phone numbers and mobile numbers of the leadership team and the board of directors (if your role includes working with these). Obtain a list from your colleagues, or start compiling one yourself.

Who's who?

One very important thing for you to do early on in your new role is to work out who everyone is. Get hold of whatever organisation structure diagram you can find. If your predecessor has done their job well, they will have included a copy in their handover notes. If they haven't, ask your boss – or the human resources department – for this. If there isn't one available, start compiling one and get it printed and up on your wall as soon as you possibly can. It doesn't have to be fancy – just use the basic organisation chart tool within Word if you have to, or draw it up on a piece of paper – but having something that identifies who works where, and for whom, is vital. You can then issue this to new starters to help them too. Use this experience as a starting point for creating (or feeding into) a handbook that can be given to all new staff.

Check it through with your boss and ask if you have the reporting lines marked up correctly. More than likely they will be pleased that you are using your initiative in creating something that is badly needed within the organisation, so you will be getting some 'brownie points' straight away for being so pro-active. Once you have an organisation chart in front of you, start working your way around it – getting to know who everyone is and checking out their roles and responsibilities within the organisation: who works with who, in which teams, and reports to whom?

If you have a staff photo list, print it out and stick it on your wall, and use it alongside the structure diagram – or insert the various photos direct into the organisation chart. If there doesn't seem to be a centralised staff photo list, create one of those too! Check with whoever creates your staff security badges and ask for access to the photos of staff. Creating a list of staff names with their photos will be a godsend to you in the first few weeks in a new role, as you can look up the person you just chatted with at lunchtime and work out their relationship to your role – and again, it can become part of the handbook for new staff.

Keep a list of important people, and be sure to keep it up-to-date

You will find that building a database of dignitaries and invited guests for all your major events will take time but, most importantly, you need to remember that whatever list you create should be reviewed and amended year in, year out. So start compiling a list of VIPs and dignitaries from the moment you start your role.

The people outside of the company who were deemed 'important' five years ago may not be the most appropriate individuals to invite to an event taking place now, when the organisation, the staffing, perhaps even your products or services (and often that person's involvement and interest in the company) have all moved on in different directions.

Make some very important new 'buddies'

Whenever you start a new job, one of the first things you need to do is to meet, greet and get to know a particular team of best buddies – the people who will help you out at the crucial times throughout the coming years. Generally, this team consists of:

- The reprographics expert – in charge of the copying facilities.

- The site officer/caretaker – the holder of the keys to the building and the access codes for the security system, and the person who can put up signage for events and reserve parking spaces for any important guests.

- The IT expert – who can reboot the server or kick-start a faulty laptop at a moment's notice.

- The chef/catering manager – the key to everyone's stomachs, including refreshments for meetings.

- The receptionist(s) – who will usually be the font of all knowledge about the whole organisation.

Seek out these people, find out their names, memorise them and make friendly working relationships with them. There will be times when you desperately need their assistance –when a huge amount of copying simply HAS to be done at late notice, when the building needs to be kept open til late one evening in order to help you get a tender or bid completed on time, when the computer network breaks down just a few minutes before a vital meeting, when a large party of visitors descend on the organisation and are in need of refreshments, or when you are waiting for a special VIP visitor but you don't want to be seen hanging around waiting for them in the foyer of the building.

Like I've said, make friends with these people. Add them to your personal Christmas card list, give them a bottle of wine or a box of chocolates on their birthday, bring them back a little 'silly something' from your holiday abroad – and get on their good side. Thank them for their assistance and always let them know how much you appreciate their help. This is most definitely not a case of sucking up to people – this is a case of rapidly building good working relationships with the individuals who will be vital to you throughout your role in this organisation.

Always thank your buddies for their assistance and let them know how much you appreciate their help. Always give credit where it is due and make sure your colleagues get recognition from others for their efforts – for example, ask the boss to say a special 'thank you' to them during a staff meeting or find a way to praise them in the organisation newsletter.

Ultimately, everyone in the organisation will be important to you in some way, but these five people will tend to be amongst the most important – they are your new 'A Team', your best buddies...

Then build working relationships with everyone else

Build your relationships with everyone in the company slowly and at a steady pace. Everything we do has a knock-on effect further down the line...

Whilst I was delivering a training programme in Kenya in 2014 I talked with a Kenyan speaker (Mr Bonnie Kim) who had previously been a cleaner in one company whilst putting himself through a college course. Whilst he worked at that company, the Managing Director had always made a point of chatting with ALL members of staff that he met within the building, including Bonnie. On finishing his college course, Bonnie then went on to build his motivational speaking business and writing books – and after several successful years of running his own company, he actually appointed the MD to come and work for him! This was, Bonnie said, an extreme demonstration of the importance of building great working relationships with EVERYONE at every level, because you never know what the future may hold...

This applies both inside your company and out – simple things like building a good working relationship during the year with a stationery supplier will undoubtedly pay dividends when you are asked to source something at extremely short notice – because you have nurtured that relationship, you should be able to persuade them to send an urgent item to you via courier to meet that vital deadline, and still negotiate a lower price with them.

All of these things can make a difference to someone, somewhere. Let it be you that makes it happen.

Take it gently

A word of caution on starting in your new role: I've met a few PAs in the past who have started at a new job by blasting their way in, as if through concrete. They have barged in on conversations, shoved their point forward in discussions and pushed themselves to the forefront in an effort to try to gain the immediate recognition and respect of their colleagues.

One PA who joined a company where I was working told me on her first day that she wanted to make it clear that she was 'a force to be reckoned with', and that when she asked for something to be done (on behalf of the team of professors for whom she worked) she wanted everyone on the staff to know that it 'jolly well ought to be done, sharp-ish'. My hackles went straight up at this, and I would strongly recommend against holding these sort of views and going in with this sort of approach.

Admittedly, being a PA / EA is not the best role in which to make yourself lots of lovely fluffy cuddly friends within the workforce. If you are looking to make lots of great friends at work, you are in the wrong place I'm afraid. You should aim to be *friendly* with your colleagues, but not aim for friendships. If a friendship actually does develop then consider that a bonus (and a hindrance at times!), but do realise that being a PA / EA does mean that you need to be forceful with some people (chasing deadlines, insisting on their providing documents at short notice, turning down their requests for meetings or to be put through on the phone, etc.)

As much as you should be acting in a friendly manner towards your colleagues you would definitely do well not to go out of your way during your first few days (or at any time, for that matter) to make any enemies. If you are starting a new job, in the early days, you are likely to meet other people in other roles who know much more about the organisation than you do, and who will not appreciate being bullied or harassed.

Make a slower, stronger, sleeker approach to building working relationships with your fellow staff. After all, if things go well you could be in this role and working alongside these people for many years to come, so work on making a really positive start.

Be ready to learn

Of major importance is that you are ready to LEARN in your new role – and to allow others to learn from you when they are new in their role. None of us knows SO much that we can start a new job without having to find things out from others – and we should ALWAYS be prepared to take on new learning. Take being new to your job as an opportunity to start learning as much as you can. You are going to be working for an Executive who has presumably worked hard to make their way up the career ladder to where they are now: learn from them. You need to understand a certain amount of what they know, if you are to be able to successfully deal with their telephone calls and correspondence, to make small talk with their visitors, or to produce their presentations for meetings and events.

The final thing you need to do at the very start of your new role is to:

Set up regular meetings with your boss

I would estimate that you will need to formally spend time with your boss for at least an hour per week at the beginning of your new role – maybe longer. This is so that you and they can discuss the forthcoming meetings, priorities and actions required of you, the recurring tasks coming up, the new projects on the horizon, and for you to get to know their working practices as quickly as possible.

You should also aim to use this time to find out more from them about the organisation and their role within it. Schedule a meeting in their calendar and yours – and make sure that it happens – each week.

Some Executives may baulk at this idea when you are so new in your role: it is often a trust issue, in that they don't know you very well yet and may not wish to share so much work detail yet – but having these meetings and showing an active interest in what they are doing in order that you can support them to the best of your ability should start to have a positive effect on any trust issues.

As time goes by and you develop within your role, the length of this meeting time can reduce – but you should still have some time with your boss each week to go through the forthcoming priorities and diary dates, and to discuss projects and tasks.

"WELCOME TO THE CIRCUS. COME IN AND TAKE YOUR SEATS"

4. WELCOMING EVERYONE TO THE CENTRE OF THE ACTION

The Ticket Collector: acts as Front of House

In small organisations, the PA / EA may well be the only full-time administrative staff member and may also serve as the Receptionist. In larger organisations, the PA / EA is more likely to be part of a team of PAs / EAs and other administrators. Either way, whilst we support the Executives of the organisation, we serve as the Front of House – the first main port of call for visitors and callers to our Executive's office.

As such, we are the eyes, ears and mouthpiece of the organisation which puts us in a great position to act as Ambassadors for our bosses (and for the role of PA / EA – more on that later!), as we see, meet, speak to, and deal with our customers or clients, service providers, guests, VIP visitors.

For many of these people, we might be the ONLY person they have contact with when they phone in or visit the building – they may not need to go any further, as we are able to deal with their request at the first point of contact. So what you say and do, and how you act, to a visitor or caller can have an enormous effect on the business.

It might seem corny, but making a point of smiling when you answer the telephone really does make a difference – the caller can pick up on it.

It is vital that whatever 'front line' role we are in, whether being on Reception or being the Executive's Assistant and taking all their calls, or greeting visitors to a meeting with our boss – we should put forward the best image we can of the organisation and ensure that we know what the company's latest plans are in case we are asked any questions. For example, if the organisation is currently advertising for a role, potential candidates may try to get find out some information from you which might help them with a job application, or if the organisation has submitted a tender for work, the receiving organisation may want to check some facts and figures, and may get in touch. If you are the person they speak to, you need to sound knowledgeable about the organisation – or at least, if you know nothing about the tender, you need to sound capable enough of finding out who they need to speak to.

In the past, I've been saddened to meet several Reception staff who have had little or no interest in what their organisation does – and when confronted with a question from a visitor or a caller, they would just gamely send the person in my direction, with an "I don't know, ask Angela" rather than "I'll find out". They have not asked me the query themselves and they have not found out the answer – so this has meant whenever the same query is asked of them, they have once more said "I don't know" and passed the person on to me again.

Not only has this wasted my time, but it has wasted the time of the caller or visitor, and it has made the organisation look bad. Nobody expects the Reception staff to know the answer to *everything*, but it really helps give a good impression of the organisation if the person who answers the main phone lines or is seated at a desk in Reception has a good idea of what's going on, and doesn't just sit there looking or sounding clueless.

I've always advocated that, whatever your level of responsibility within an organisation – if a member of the public, a customer, a client, a supplier, ANYONE – asks you a question, you would be far better placed to say something like "That's a good question. I'm not sure of the answer – let me go and find out for you." Then put the caller on hold – or take their number and promise to call them back shortly – or ask the visitor to take a seat. Then go and do what you say – find out – and let them know the result.

Don't just blindly pass them on to someone else. Who knows, their question might be something that the very next person who calls you also asks. And do please make sure you get back to them: one thing I cannot bear is when someone tells me that they will call me back about my query but they then don't actually do it.

Please note: I am not saying "learn everybody else's job in the organisation and never put calls through to anyone else". What I am saying is "take an active interest in the roles of others in the organisation, and in what the company is doing, new projects, new plans, advertising, new products, etc. so that you can be better informed and can assist with queries."

It is a question of being sensible, and furthering your own knowledge within your role so that you can answer queries with confidence and put forward a better view of your organisation to the outside world.

Your office is the centrepiece of the circus – it is the circus ring

In your role as PA / EA to the leader of an organisation, you will almost automatically be making a difference to the work and lives of those around you, pretty much by simply being there. You will ease the lives of others by arranging much needed meetings with your boss, handling queries from those who have no idea where else to go with their questions, sorting out problems that don't 'fit' within other departments and dealing with students, parents and other concerned parties in a professional and methodical manner.

For my part, I've always know that my PA roles were really important – providing the vital link between everyone in the organisation, whether they be chairmen, chief executives, directors, principals, professors, deputy vice chancellors, leadership teams, professors, committees, tutors, students, their families, governing bodies, sponsors and so on. I am really proud that what I did on a day-to-day basis was to provide a first class level of support and I got great satisfaction from knowing that my efforts were making a difference. My hope is that you can gain that feeling of satisfaction in your role too – enjoying what you do, feeling appreciated, and knowing that you too make a difference.

After the chairman, chief executive and managing director, their assistants are quite possibly the most important staff members when it comes to running the organisation. You might attempt to counter this by pointing out that you don't build or make the product or provide the service that your company does, and that you are "only an administrator". DON'T! The PA or EA in any organisation is the glue that holds everything together, the central cog in the machinery, the conduit through which the electricity flows. As the Executive/Manager is linked with all the departments of the company, so are we, which puts us in a unique position amongst the staff, because we know the confidential 'ins and outs' of the whole organisation.

We are also in a key position to influence the decision-makers on a huge range of issues. We are the Executive's 'third arm', and our role is to support them in whatever they do. This means we need to know a great deal about what they know, what they do and how they do it in order to work well with them and provide the support that they need.

To be a great PA / EA we need to create good working relationships with the staff in every department. They need to know that we are supporting them in their jobs through the support we give to the Executive. They also need to know that you are acting on behalf of the Executive, and that if you are asking them to do something, this usually means that you are asking them on behalf of the Executive so they need to respond appropriately.

As a PA, EA or secretary you are, effectively, an extension of the Executive, their second voice within the organisation. By creating and maintaining good relationships with the staff, and by demonstrating your enthusiasm and commitment for your role, you can also be a good motivator to others. People from elsewhere in the company will naturally gravitate towards you as the "go to person" when they have a query. By soaking up as much information and knowhow about your Executive as you can, you can provide a greater level of support throughout the organisation. Make the most of this – and be the benchmark by which other assistants are measured. Inspire others to aim for excellence in what they do and be a role model for them.

"AND IN THE AUDIENCE TONIGHT, WE HAVE
THE JONES FAMILY. MR JONES WORKS FOR
THE ABC CORPORATION AND MRS JONES
TEACHES AT THE LOCAL PRIMARY SCHOOL..."

5. CONTACTS LISTS

The Audience: the importance of maintaining a great Contacts list

A major element of the role of PA / EA is to protect your Executive or manager from others and to protect their time. This includes putting through the phone calls which they need to take (and stop those that they don't). You will also be permitting appropriate visitors to their offices at appropriate times (whilst fielding off all the other requests for meetings which ought to be dealt with by somebody else in the organisation).

Key to your success in these areas will be to have a firm grip on who your boss knows, who they want to see, who they don't want to hear from, and being able to fend off everyone else in a polite manner – whilst being firm when necessary in order to deal with unwanted or persistent callers (we'll come to those in another chapter!!).

Get to know everyone your boss knows

Everyone your boss knows is someone that you need to know too, so you need to obtain contact details for everyone they meet.

Get to know your boss's contacts list inside out.

Whenever your Executive attends a conference or large meeting, ask them to gather business cards from the people they meet and talk with. Collate these in a shared contacts folder in Outlook that both you and your Executive can access.

Similarly, each time a visitor attends your office for a meeting with your Executive, ask them for one of their business cards and add them into your contacts folder – and if you've served them with a drink, make a note of what they had (whether they prefer tea or coffee, caffeinated vs. decaffeinated, whether they take milk, sugar, sweeteners, etc.).

You will impress them no end – especially if they only visit your offices infrequently – if, when they enter the office, you can greet them and say correctly, 'You like your coffee with milk and two sugars, right?' It's one of those little things that shows you have paid attention and that you care. It also demonstrates that you are acting professionally in trying to ensure that everyone gets a good welcome and takes away a positive image of the organisation.

If you have time, add photos to the folder for all the people for whom you have phone numbers. This should be easy for the members of staff at your own organisation as there is likely to be a folder on your computer network containing all their photos. (Remember the rule of thumb: if there isn't one, make one!) Adding photos means that, if your Executive / Manager is using a smartphone linked to Outlook, the contact's photo will be displayed on the phone when they call, providing an instant visual reminder of who is calling.

This is very useful if you have a large number of staff or your boss has lots of contacts around the world – seeing someone's face before answering their call can really help with memory recall.

Keep track of last conversations and personal details

Keep notes on essential contacts in Outlook – what they do, where they are based, any personal information they share and a couple of facts about your last conversation. These are 'god-send' bits of information for you (or your boss) to feed into your next conversations with them – it will show them that you were really and make them feel treasured and remembered.

If you or the boss can call someone and bring into the conversation a question about something that they mentioned on their last visit or call, then you and your Executive and your organisation will stand out as caring and interested listeners.

Another useful side to knowing the names of all your Executive's main contacts is that it will be quicker and easier for you to spot cold-callers who call and pretend to be known to them in order to be put through on the phone.

Be prepared for your contacts list to be fairly expansive

In several of my PA roles throughout my career, I could go home in the evening with my head reeling from the sheer number of tasks I had been involved in during the day. Added to my list of tasks would be the huge number of people with whom I had worked that day – sometimes, I swear that my contacts list was longer than the local phone directory.

During my last role I was in regular contact with the entire staff of the school where I worked, along with the pupils, parents, governors, sponsors, the local community, local councillors, visitors, press, marketing companies, suppliers – not to mention the many peripatetic teachers, supply agencies, royalty, sports figures, TV weathermen and chefs, builders, project planners, uniform suppliers, local shops, and many more who frequented our school or contacted us each day. In addition my boss, the Principal of the school, was Chair of the local Headteachers' group and was a member of a group of international speakers – as well the author of two successful books. He was frequently called upon by local and national newspapers, and his contact list almost rivalled mine in length and breadth.

Directly preceding this role, I worked at a Management Consultancy / Executive Search organisation where I had daily contact with our 25 offices across the UK and Europe, in addition to all of the other staff in our building (including a team of 30 or more recruiters) plus many of the company's contacts in any of the organisations where we placed candidates. Working at an international seaport in Ireland, I had a contacts list of several hundred shipping companies and their various employees with whom I was in regular contact, as well as other ports around the country, members of the Government's Marine Department, various shipping associations and groups, and a whole range of contacts with the local press – as well as all of the various companies for whom we shipped products into and out of Ireland.

Depending on the nature and size of your company, you could potentially have an enormous contacts list – so talk with your Executive about this, gather together the business cards they have received, and get to creating a list. You might find some software useful – there are various apps now available that will scan business cards and populate a database for you.

Print a paper copy of your contacts list

Whatever system you use to create your list of contacts, make sure that every now and again you print a copy of it to keep it locked away somewhere safely in case the ICT systems all go down and you can't get to your contacts list on screen. At least with a paper copy of the list you'd be able to make a few vital phone calls. Later in this book I'll talk about creating a Purple Folder full of vital things for your role – your contacts list is one of these items.

This chapter is symbolised by two Circus mainstays: the Safety Net and the Acrobatic Duo. You are the boss's support net. To support him, you need to trust each other.

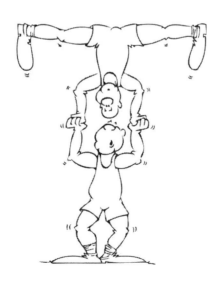

6. BEING A TRUSTED SUPPORTER TO YOUR BOSS

The nature of your role is that you are a direct extension of your boss – their second voice, their third arm within the organisation. You are also their support net, you hold them safely as they go about their daily business of running the circus.

At the start of your working relationship, you both need to build trust in each other pretty quickly if you are to support them well. They need to trust you enough to hand you work of a particular level and to trust you with confidential matters – and to trust your judgement. You need to trust that you have the skills to fulfil the role and trust in the way in which your Executive is leading the organisation.

Be behind them in what they do

You need to be behind what your boss stands for. Not every single little tiny thing. You can never be that sure of everything they do. But most things – the fundamental things – what they stand for, what they believe in, what their aims and goals are for the school, what their vision is for the future of the college, what changes and innovations they want to bring to the university.

You need to support, respect and believe in your Executive and what they do. If you aren't in agreement with what they are working to achieve, then I'm afraid you are working in the wrong job. How could you possibly provide the best support to someone if you aren't behind them on what they do?

If you find that you only believe in half of what they do, then you must be spending 50% of your time disagreeing with them. That's not going to be conducive to a good relationship or to providing excellent support for them – so my rule of thumb is that you need to believe in your boss for at least 75% of what they say and do.

Build a great working relationship

In order to provide the best support possible to your boss, you need to believe in them, and by doing this, you can develop a fantastic working relationship with them. This doesn't mean you are going to be 'best buds', but it does mean that you trust each other wholeheartedly and each understands the other.

There are four main stages to your working relationship with your boss.

1. A telling relationship

This generally occurs in the early stages of your role, and also in some junior roles, although there are some bosses who continue in this vein for much longer. During this phase, your Executive will tell you things: they will look at a situation, make a decision, share the outcome with you and tell you what they need you to do.

It is a necessary phase as it informs you of what is needed, to what standard and when. However, it is a stage that you can, and should, grow out of – after a while you should be developing these skills and decision-making processes for yourself. Once you have moved beyond the telling relationship stage, it can feel quite strange to return to it if you change jobs because you will have started to manage your own workload more.

2. An explaining relationship

This is a little further into your working relationship when your Executive trusts you and has taken you into their confidence, so they will start to explain to you why they have made certain decisions. This builds your relationship to a more detailed level, giving you much more of an understanding of what is required in your role, including the whys and the wherefores, rather than just being informed that something needs to be done. This can prove very useful when working on a new task or project, when your Executive needs additional commitment from you or when they want you on their side to assist in 'selling' an idea to other staff.

This can be a great phase to go through: you will learn a great deal when your boss explains what they mean, how they are thinking and the bigger picture as to where things are going. It is the perfect environment for you to look at your own skills and see what you need to improve in order to fit with the information and understanding that you are now gaining of the organisation. As your working relationship with your Executive develops further, it is important that you keep asking questions, finding out more and learning in greater detail. This is what will set you apart from the other administrators in your organisation, and because you are continually learning about the institution and how your role can make a difference.

3. A consulting relationship

This stage brings together the best elements of both you and your Executive. It is when they start asking you for your thoughts on various issues, and you make joint decisions between you. Reaching this stage with your manager shows that they hold you in great trust, recognise your expertise in what you do and believe that you are working with them in partnership

4. An empowering relationship

This is when your Executive empowers you to take free rein over what you do and how you handle situations, allowing you to make necessary decisions without consulting them. This requires complete trust on both sides of the working relationship. Your Executive has confidence that you have the skills and abilities to handle this level of additional responsibility, and faith that you will represent them and speak on their behalf in the mannerisms and style that they need you to.

It is vital that you see your working relationship with your boss as a two-way street.

Learn to speak freely with your boss

Whilst you should be aiming to have an Empowering relationship with them, the other side of having a great relationship with your Executive requires that you need to have the courage to speak freely to them on important matters – and not just that they offer you the space to speak. Of course, if you tell your boss something they don't want to hear, they may not want to listen to you. But if you broach the subject with them sensitively, by starting with something along the lines of *"There is something that I think you need to be aware of..."* or *"May I tell you how I see something?"* they are more likely to be receptive of your words.

Relay their message professionally

Executives, generally, don't hesitate in telling people exactly how they feel... through you. They will be relying on you to appropriately deal with people and when they say to you "Tell so-and-so that" followed by some request or comment, it is your role as their assistant to re-word the verbiage and get your boss's message across professionally. You are an extension of your Executive and it is imperative that this fact remains at the forefront of your every move.

*****

Support for you is also incredibly important

While we're looking at the idea of your being your boss's support net – make sure you find a support net of your own. Every PA / EA deserves to have someone they can turn to for assistance.

Mentoring has been "something that management does" for a good long while now – and is slowly becoming more and more popular further down the ranks of an organisation. Make it something you participate in – find yourself a mentor to work with, and as your experience in your role grows, go on to offer yourself as a mentor to someone else.

A really important part of coping with the stresses and strains of a busy role is looking after your mental health: giving yourself time off properly when you take annual leave, taking adequate rest breaks during the day, eating well (but sensibly!), and having someone to share things with: so do yourself a favour and go find yourself a mentor.

No matter what stage you are at in your career, having a mentor you can talk to and who will give you an outside perspective on your experience, can be invaluable.

Why should you get into mentoring?

Having someone who has "been there, done that" in their own career which is similar in certain ways to your own, whom you can call upon for help and guidance, can make all the difference between doing an OK job and doing a GREAT job.

With no specific qualification required (within the UK at least) to become a PA or EA, there is also no one single textbook or set curriculum for us to follow to ensure that we are doing well in our roles.

In a survey I conducted on LinkedIn in 2013, more than 60% of respondents in PA and EA roles had drifted into their role from somewhere else, without having first built up their administrative skills in lower level roles.

Since then, the 2015 Hays / Executive Secretary "What makes a successful PA?" survey revealed that 72% of employers believe that their PA / EA should have formal qualifications – this is shown by the number of adverts for PA and EA roles where having a degree is listed as an "essential" or "desirable" qualification for the role – and only 27% of public sector and 35% of private sector PAs took up their roles straight from school. The growing perception among both employers and the PAs / EAs themselves is that we must increase our qualifications. All well and good – but where are the degree level programmes that will best qualify us for the role of PA / EA?

In the absence of these, it is imperative that we each learn our role from someone who knows what the role is like, and has some level of experience in being a successful PA or EA, hence: get a mentor!

10 things you can gain from a good mentor

    i.   **Credibility for you and your role.** The best mentors have credibility and personal success in the area where they offer support – and then help their mentees develop specific skills or qualities, or help them reach important decisions. This doesn't mean that they have all the answers – they will help you find the best answers from your own thinking, with their support.

ii.   **A positive role model.** With a good mentor, you can learn a lot from watching how they behave in any particular situation. Good mentors will also look out for experiences, or even create situations in which their mentees can become involved to learn new things, for example, providing a look behind the scenes or a glimpse at how other people live or do things.

iii. **Someone who is interested in you as an individual.** A mentoring relationship is a very personal one, so please share your hopes and dreams, so they can help you in a way that meets your personal best interest.

iv.   **An opportunity to learn from their experiences and insights.** Hearing openly from them about how they have handled mistakes or failures can be where the biggest lessons are learned and where you can build your own resilience for dealing with challenges.

v.   **The chance to ask questions** – and be asked questions yourself – so that you can think through situations and draw out the consequences of the various choices or courses of action you can take. Learning from someone else's wisdom can help with your own decision making.

vi.   **A sounding board.** You can benefit greatly from the opportunity of having a good mentor listen to you, allowing you to explore your thoughts and ideas openly. This will often help unravel your thinking and gain insights about a situation as you share your concerns.

vii. **A fresh perspective.** One of the benefits of working with a mentor is that a good mentor will often provide their mentee with a fresh perspective on an issue, often having the clarity of distance from an issue or problem that's needed to provide objective feedback. They can also hold up a 'mirror' to you to see what your behaviour looks like to others.

viii. **Helpful feedback.** Not all of the feedback we receive from others is helpful. A good mentor knows this and will deliver feedback in a way that will help you gain insight to further develop specific qualities or skills.

ix.   **Acknowledgement of your achievements.** Highlighting achievements you might have forgotten can help build confidence, whilst celebrating your successes.

x.   **Offers of advice, if you ask for it.** It can be very tempting to just jump in and offer advice before someone has actually asked for it. Being a sounding board for you, then asking questions to draw out the consequences of various actions is always more empowering than advising someone on what to do.

What might you want to work on with a mentor?

You should be the person to drive where you mentoring takes you – so go in with a clear goal that you want to look at. You might choose to look at your route to success, for example, by examining:

- How does your life look like? – your background
- Which are the most important events in your life?
- What do you do with your time – any interests?
- How do you relate to your work?
- Which are your strengths and weaknesses?
- Where are you today and where do you want to be tomorrow?

This can help you become more goal conscious in terms of how you can achieve what you want to do, choice conscious (looking at whether you make your own choices or allow or expect others to make choices for you) and self-conscious about who you are and how others see you.

How to find a mentor

To find a mentor, you might look to someone from elsewhere in your career, someone you looked up to, perhaps – or a PA / EA in another part of your organisation – or another organisation entirely. You could contact a PA / EA network or association in your country to see if they are running a mentoring scheme – or if you are involved in (or set up!) a localised network of PAs and EAs in your area, you might consider setting up a mentoring scheme amongst the members of the network, to assist each other.

A circular group of mentoring could be beneficial for everyone involved, with just four or five members – each mentoring someone else within the group…

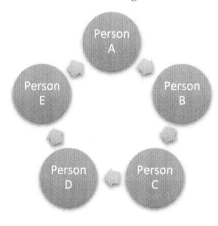

Or you might contact a PA or EA who has won an award for their work and ask if they might consider being your mentor for a period of time. Look through PA magazines and websites to find out names and details – connect with them on LinkedIn, and make an approach…

Points to note

Whichever way you do it, and whoever you find as your mentor, make the most of the relationship. Don't pay it lip-service.

Turn up for your mentoring sessions with notes of something you want to discuss – it is best if you can inform your mentor of the issue in advance of the meeting so that they can be prepared. And meetings don't have to be face-to-face real life meetings: you could use Skype or any other form of video conferencing – or just a phone call – to virtually 'meet' and discuss something. You can also use email, although it is not as immediate for responses and doesn't really allow for real-time conversations.

Ideally, your mentor will be able to share their knowledge, skills, values, perspectives and expertise. This should be a two-way thing: make sure you share yours too, so that you develop each other.

The arrangement might be for just a short period to assist you with a particular issue or skill at work – or you might choose to extend the relationship for a longer period. Calls, emails and/or meetings every one or two months might be more than sufficient – or, if your mentor is able to offer the time, more often. It all depends on what you need, what they can offer, what financial implications are involved, and the time and commitment that both parties can give to it.

Good mentoring can go a long way in furthering your development as a great PA / EA, and to support you as you grow within your role – it can be richly rewarding, providing exceptional learning experiences and expand your awareness, insight and perspective.

So, go on, find yourself a mentor – or offer your services to another PA / EA to be their mentor – and add this to your list of bankable assets.

GUARD YOUR TERRITORY

7. KEEPING 'UN-WANTEDS' AT BAY

Being a Lion-Tamer: guarding your Executive's time from unnecessary visitors and cold-callers

Be proud to be a gate-keeper: it should not be a derogatory term!

We are 'Gate Keepers' for our bosses: we decide who we let into their office or who to put through on the phone. We protect our Executives' time. It is a very important part of our role.

We may find ourselves being 'pumped' for information at times – so, as a rule of thumb, answer questions with just enough information to answer the question, especially when the queries relate to your boss.

Learn some polite ways to turn away visitors or callers

If your boss steps out of the office, or decides they do not want to be disturbed while they are in their office, external requests for their time should be addressed by simply stating, "He/she is unavailable at the moment" and followed up with, "may I take a message or help you?"

Long-winded answers about his/her lunch meeting with such-and-such client, or the minutiae of their diary are not necessary. People will always fill in the blanks with their own inferences, no matter how thorough or vague you are, so it is best to stick to bare minimum facts unless otherwise instructed.

Sometimes we need to tell a little white lie rather than the truth of "he told me he does not want to talk with you" – but also, in some instances it actually might be appropriate to say exactly that. It is a judgement call, depending on the situation.

If, for example, it is a colleague who is asking you to book a meeting for them which you know should be with someone else on the leadership team rather than your Executive, your first response might be "he's unavailable, but I can arrange a meeting for you with YYYY". Or you might respond "at this level, your query ought to go through YYYY before it goes further to my boss". Whichever way you choose to say anything, aim for polite, helpful and firm.

Make the most of your contacts list

Working for the leader of an organisation, it is highly likely that you will be on the receiving end of a fair number of cold-callers who want you to put them through to your Executive.

If you have created a decent contacts list with your boss you will know who they know, which will then make it easier for you to field cold-callers and marketer who call, asking for the Executive or manager on a first name basis and pretending they know them personally as a method of 'by-passing' the PA.

Do believe me that this happens – I have worked in two organisations where the sales and recruiting staff were expressly trained in methods of 'getting past the gatekeeper', to push past the PA, to belittle the assistant into putting the call through to their manager. I thought this was a horrendous tactic – and PAs worldwide agree with me.

A good PA / EA is there to prevent unwanted calls from getting through, so sales staff and recruiters would be far better positioned if they made friends with the PA / EA during their calls instead of treating us badly and expecting us to put their calls through.

I got so used to cold callers telephoning me in one role that I learnt to recognise their type of call from twenty paces… But what should you do with them?

I put this question to a group of PAs and EAs on LinkedIn, and the following is adapted from the resulting article. You may find the views and suggestions in it very useful – they come from a large number of PAs worldwide on their experiences.

Dealing with cold-callers

One classic timewaster in our role as PAs, and a vitally important person for us to 'weed out' from the calls that we put through to our Executive or manager, is the cold-caller, the salesperson, the marketer – and what to do with them.

I love cold-callers – I just couldn't eat a whole one.

Dealing with cold-callers comes up regularly during training courses and online PA networks – in particular, the type of cold-callers who think the best way to reach the managers/executives of our organisation is to blast their way past the PA or receptionist with lies and counter-lies. PAs at my training courses have confirmed that this is an approach they have come across in both the corporate world and in education.

Cold-callers can be the bane of our lives, as it is usually our role to be the gatekeeper between the outside world and our Executive/Manager.

Over the years, I have heard from many salespeople trying to reach the executive of my organisation by telephone in order to sell their products – many of these being services or items which have no relevance to our organisation, and many others who are pitching to completely the wrong person. Some callers will actually give details of their products, services or organisation while they are speaking to me, but a large number have attempted to use bullying or derogatory techniques to try to shame me into thinking that I am 'just a lowly PA' and that the best thing I could do would be to put them straight through to my manager, thank you very much.

Others still have lied outright, saying that they met my boss at an event recently and he asked them to call him – which I always check so that I can report back to them when the boss says he's never heard of them. He retains all business cards from the people he meets, but he certainly doesn't have theirs.

Some cold-callers will use ridiculously stupid tactics – I once took a call from someone who claimed to be my chief executive's GP, but I already knew the details of his GP's surgery, and my phone's screen showed that the caller's telephone number was from elsewhere in the country.

Some callers have blatantly lied in an attempt to reach the boss, often mistakenly believing that he is the one-and-only decision-maker with whom they need to speak, while others will claim to be personal friends.

One key to handling cold-callers is to know your manager very well. Get to know what type of work he deals with, whom he deals with and the names of people he knows on a personal basis, as well as his business contacts. Take responsibility for storing and cataloguing the business cards that he receives – remind him to collect them when on his travels and to give them to you.

When he does, ask for details from him on each person so that you can note these down. After all, if you know who he met recently and would be interested in hearing from, you are well prepared for when they call – and equally, you know who to turn away when they claim to be a personal or private contact.

We therefore need to be able to spot a cold-caller at 20 paces and have some techniques for how to deal with them.

The typical cold-caller is selling something, whether this is a product, service or a person (many recruiters will try to sell you a new member of staff who they believe is vital for your organisation).

They will call and ask you to put them through to your manager – often without telling you who they are, where they are from or the nature of the call.

Very few will admit that they are salespeople. When asked questions, they will be evasive or abrupt, sometimes even rude, in an attempt to get past you. Often they will imply that the call is personal or private, or highly confidential. As a confidential PA, though, they really ought to realise that you are the person they need to speak with!

When receiving a call from a number I don't recognise, I often pause for a second to click the Internet Explorer icon on my computer screen before answering the phone. In the first few seconds of the call I can type the phone number into Google to see if any useful information comes up, including whether they are listed on the internet as a nuisance caller.

Another tip is to get your manager's approval that all his calls have to go through you – and, in particular, all of his outside calls. This means no one in the organisation should be able to put a call through to him directly – they must put it through you first. In this way, you can immediately connect your boss with the important people – governors, board members, staff, genuine contacts, etc. – and hold off the others, saying that you need to know the caller's reason for calling before your manager will take the call.

When putting calls through, give your manager a quick précis of what you have been told by the caller, and remind him on a regular basis to let you know afterwards if a caller didn't speak to them on that topic but on something else. This not only helps you to stay on top of the various projects which your manager is working on, but it also informs you when a cold-caller has got through the net, so you know not to put that person through again.

I often think that if the salespeople could only do their market research better, then they would save us a huge amount of time – and themselves too! If they could aim their calls towards the most appropriate person at an organisation, rather than just trying to bulldoze their way to the manager / executive/chief executive/chairman, it would make everything so much easier.

I've received so many calls about recruitment which should have been directed to the HR manager rather than my boss, so many calls about corporate transport which should have been directed to the person who actually books corporate transport, but the salespeople concerned have been taught aggressive sales tactics that convince them that the only person at an organisation who can make a decision about anything is the head of that organisation.

In fact, most discussions about suppliers or service providers are held at other management levels, by the people responsible for using those services. In the vast majority of cases, it is only when proposals have been factored, costed, compared with existing providers and weighed up fully that the proposal will make its way to the head of the organisation for board approval.

From my various PA contacts, I've heard some absolute horror stories of cold-callers and salespeople who have stalked bosses or their assistants, pushed their way past receptionists, blagged their way into the building and made their way to the boss's office, or out-and-out lied on the phone in order to reach the head of the organisation – all in the name of making an unsolicited cold call.

One salesperson apparently turned up at an organisation and hung around reception at the end of the day, then ambushed the chief executive as he was leaving the building. The chief executive curtly told the salesman, 'You either deal with my PA or no one – do not attempt to deal with me again.'

PAs around the world have shared their advice on dealing with cold-callers who insist they can speak with no one but the boss:

- 'I've told cold-callers: "All of the CEO's calls are taken by me. If you won't talk to me about it, I'm afraid I cannot put you through to him. If you will let me know what you are calling about, it may be more appropriate that your call goes to another member of staff who has responsibility for that area, and I'll try to put you through to them." This generally works, and I can then redirect their call as appropriate.'

- 'If a salesperson is upfront and honest, I will help direct them to the correct person. The latest pitch I've been getting is that my manager indicated an interest in their product online and asked that they get in touch with her, which I know is a total lie, and they call back every two or three weeks, thinking that I'm not intelligent enough to recognise them and their lame pitch. If my manager was interested in an online product, then I'd be the one contacting them about it.'

- 'I ask the caller politely to recognise that part of my job is to screen the boss's calls and that I will not be able to put them through until I know what the call is about and I can vet their call.'

- 'I've been on both sides of the desk – buyer and seller. As a buyer, I have the experience and knowledge to notice when a product has potential to help my company, and will be happy to talk to a sales rep. As a seller, I preferred to first invest the time and research to learn what problems my product could offer to solve in an organisation, and then to focus on earning the right to both talk to and learn from the person who will benefit from the solution.'

- 'I think a lot of salespeople underestimate how much we actually know about the business our CEO is handling and what we need at that time. You are better off working directly with the PA – but keep in mind that a sales call (to us) is still a sales call. If we have a need, you have treated us with respect for our time and you aren't pushy, we will probably come to you first when we have a need.'

- 'Bottom of my list are sales calls from someone trying to use the CEO's first name. "Is Fred there?" Really! If they knew Fred so well, they'd have his mobile phone number or his direct line. Those calls just make me laugh. They can keep calling me – Fred will still be in a never-ending meeting.'

My own standard response to anyone cold-calling within my last role was that all of our strategic leadership group, including the Manager, were very pressed for time and didn't make decisions on any product or service on the strength of a phone call. If the caller would please send an email with all the necessary details regarding their company, their product or service, their website and their contact details, then I would pass it on to the most relevant person in the academy. If that person then wanted to take things further, they would contact the caller. I asked the callers not to chase, but to accept that a nil response from us after a fortnight would mean that we did not require their services.

Some callers crop up on a regular basis, ringing year in, year out. This applies across all industries, including education. On the UK Academies PA network, which I chaired for five years, members regularly reported to each other when a known cold-caller started 'doing the rounds again' – every year we received calls from the 'Government Initiatives Office' (which is nothing to do with the government), 'St James House' (nothing to do with royalty) and the 'Parliamentary Yearbook' (surprise, surprise – nothing to do with parliament), all of whom wished to urgently speak with our Principals or Head teachers on a personal, private matter.

The actual purpose of each of their calls was to gain the Head's ear about paying for marketing space or editorial space in their publication. Given that we were all state-funded schools with very small marketing budgets (if any), most of our Heads didn't want to be bothered with this sort of call and didn't wish to advertise in the publications, so we PAs worked to stop the calls from getting through.

Year on year, PAs reported to the network that callers from these organisations were even using the same script which they attempted to read out over the phone. Year on year, we all turned them away and notified each other via the network, so that other academies could be forewarned about their imminent calls.

One of my PA connections contacted me a few years ago saying, 'I just had a caller who wants to speak to my MD about "Her Majesty's 85th birthday celebration". I asked if this call was an invitation to an event (knowing that it was not). "No, no!" said the caller. He could not speak with me – he must speak with my managing director personally. The caller was aggressive, supercilious and rude. I have had dealings with this "organisation" before. They must think we are morons. I have tipped off all our directors. If he calls back, I shall be having a bit of fun!'

Another PA who made regular visits to Buckingham Palace received the exact same call and asked her cold-caller which office they were in, as she might be able to pop in to see them that afternoon to discuss whatever they were calling about, before she made her way to the palace for a meeting.

Needless to say, the caller became somewhat flustered and was unable to respond, then hung up the phone.

The final word on dealing with cold-callers has to go to the PA who related: 'I love cold calls: I recently told a double-glazing salesman that he should pop round to price up for me. I live on the eighth floor of a tower block.'

KEEPING ALL THE PLATES SPINNING

8. MULTI-TASKING IN EXTREMIS

The Plate Spinner: skilled at multi-tasking in extremis

How do you keep track of everything that goes on in your role – and keep all those plates spinning all at once? I'm firmly convinced that PAs are some of the busiest people on the planet. We are required to think on our feet, juggle multiple tasks and priorities, and keep track of the tiniest of details in preparation for almost any eventuality. Think about the tasks that you undertake in a supposedly 'normal' day in your office….

For example, you may have a boss who reels out a huge list of tasks all in one go, just before they leave the office. In case you haven't experienced this, let me check: have you seen the film 'The Devil Wears Prada' starring Anne Hathaway and Emily Blunt as the unfortunate down-trodden assistants at 'Runway" magazine, working for Miranda, an absolutely hideous boss played by Meryl Streep? The storyline is well known to be based on being the true life experiences of being an assistant to Anna Wintour at Vogue magazine – and whilst it gives a really awful stereotypical view of the role of the Personal / Executive Assistant, there are some great pointers for us all to learn from. The particular scene that I have in mind is where Andi, played by Anne Hathaway, is called into the office. In the space of approximately 60 seconds, she is told by the magazine's editor Miranda Priestley:

"Tell Simone I'm not going to approve that girl that she sent me for the Brazilian layout. I asked for 'clean, athletic, smiling': she sent me 'dirty, tired and paunchy'. And RSVP 'yes' to Michael Kors' party: I want the driver to drop me off at 9:30 and pick me up at 9:45 sharp. Call Natalie at Glorious Foods and tell her 'no' for the 40th time: no, I don't want dacquoise, I want tortes filled with warm rhubarb compote. Then call my ex-husband and remind him that the parent-teacher conference is at Dalton tonight. Then call my husband, ask him to meet me for dinner at that place I went to with Massimo. Tell Richard I saw the pictures that he sent for that feature on the female paratroopers and they're all so deeply unattractive. Is it impossible to find a lovely, slender, female paratrooper? Am I reaching for the stars here? Not really. Also, I need to see all the things that Nigel has pulled for Gwyneth's second cover try."

A daunting list of tasks, delivered in the space of a minute, the scene summarises the role of a busy PA / EA – multiple priorities, multiple tasks, second-guessing, anticipating what else is required, filling in the gaps, and performing memory miracles in remembering the names of contacts and who is the best person to speak to about X, Y or Z. If I was asked to name the two major skills needed by a great Personal Assistant or Executive Assistant, they would be the ability to prioritise our time and remembering things.

(As an aside, women are allegedly four times better than men at multi-tasking or switching from one task to another to another, according to scientists. Why might this be? It seemingly stems from the division of labour between the sexes, both of whom adapted to surviving the dangers of Stone Age life. In this, men went out to find an animal to kill for food, whilst the women stayed in the 'home' cave environment, nursing children, tending the fire, looking for water, foraging for berries and nuts, and protecting the children from harm from animals – they could not just focus on making clothes or finding food. That's the background of our multi-tasking abilities and behaviour.)

Research in 1956 by George Miller determined that our short term memory allows us to hold information on a certain number of topics at a time – the 'magic number 7' – which is then explained as being '7 plus or minus 2'. (Quite why this could not just be reported as 'between 5 and 9 items', I don't know, maybe '7 plus or minus 2' rolls off the tongue easier?) Anyway – if you are now, halfway through this paragraph, able to hold in your mind any 5 or more of the tasks reeled out by Miranda Priestley in her speech on the last page, very well done. It is very difficult to hear a list of fairly randomised items and remember them all afterwards. So, short of going on a 'memory mastermind' course, I can make one recommendation to you: invest in a digital pen which can record audio whilst you write. There are several out there on the market – the one I have is a Livescribe pen.

The Livescribe is teamed with a specially printed notepad (which has an array of tiny dots on it) – by tapping the pen's nib on the 'record' button at the bottom of the page before starting to write any notes, whatever I hear while I'm writing is recorded as an mp3 file – and then both the handwritten notes and the audio file can be transferred to my PC / laptop / iPad for working on them further. Various apps can further enhance this – one to translate handwriting to typed text, whilst speech recognition will have a good bash at turning the audio file into text. An integral function is that at any time in the future you can go back to any page in your notepad and double-click on a paragraph – and the pen will automatically play back to you the sounds that were recorded at that time, so you can listen back to a meeting or a lecture or a presentation months later. My particular model connects via wire to the computer – newer ones work via Wi-Fi – and they all have a several GigaByte capacity, so you really can go back to them weeks if not months later to listen to your notes. My 2GB pen can hold 200 hours of recordings, for instance.

So, picture again that scene from the film – and replay it with your trusty new digital pen in hand. Next time your boss comes to you with a list of tasks, double-tap your pen's nib on the "record" button and start making whatever notes you wish to – whatever you don't manage to capture in your notes is being safely recorded and can be played back afterwards. This helps to ensure that you don't miss anything important when frantically scribbling notes or trying to remember everything that's said to you. Digital pens are around the £100 mark – but have so many uses you will be sure to get your money's worth very quickly from them.

Prioritising your work

Very rarely does a PA / EA have the luxury of working on (and completing) one single task uninterrupted, as there will invariably be interruptions of some sort – an urgent phone call that needs to be dealt with, a message to pass on to a colleague or manager, or some sort of metaphorical fire to put out for someone on the team. Something or someone will always be put on hold, and as a great assistant you have to work out, instinctively, the best order for carrying out tasks or delegating them to another team member.

In addition, you need to be able to work out how long each task should take, in order to make sure that everything will be done by the correct deadline. For this, I'd recommend making full use of whatever software is available to you – I personally use the calendar / tasks and categories functions within Microsoft Outlook, so that I can plan my week as best as possible. You need, when planning, to leave a bit of space as there will always be additional urgent tasks that present themselves throughout each day. Quite often, getting the day's tasks done will require juggling that would put the average circus plate spinner to shame! (More on prioritising and scheduling elsewhere in this book.)

Some PAs take saving time and effort to extremes…

From my networking with PAs around the world, I'm aware of one Personal Assistant in the USA who was looking for work, and who decided to take matters into her own hands. She worked out that it would take her a fair amount of time and effort to apply for jobs, and decided to turn the situation on its head. Instead of spending her time looking for a job, she invited potential employers to find her instead – by placing an advertisement in the employment section of her local paper on the following lines:

"Are you a busy Executive with far too much work to do, and need an assistant with the strength to scale tall buildings in one leap? I've got great office skills, fantastic organisational skills, a lot of common sense, and an excellent track record. We should work together – call xxx(phone number)xxx."

She received a large number of calls, including several offers of interviews within the first day of her advert – and was able to pick and choose between them, without having to spend her own time looking for jobs and applying for them.

Whenever any of my employers have interviewed for Personal Assistants and admin staff, I have advised them to ask the interviewees about their abilities to handle multiple tasks, priorities and deadlines, to ensure that they are hiring the right people for the role. If a candidate can't do two things at once (like greet a visitor to the office whilst on a phone call), they'd be in real trouble in a PA role.

However, the ability to handle a large number of tasks and contacts while still retaining a sense of reality are skills that are gained from experience – both your own and learning from others – I don't think anybody is born with a natural tendency to be able to organise, make lists, or remember who's who in a company of a thousand people.

Boost your memory

Here are a few memory tips, to help you to deal with the multiple actions and requests on your time:

1. Make a "to do" list – and update it every day. Create a new, fresh list each week, including any items carried forward from last week. Whether it be on paper or electronic, make your list and work through it. There will always be interruptions and additional items popping up – but add them to the list and cross them off when they are completed.

2. Do small tasks straightaway – if it will take you five minutes or less, do it now to get the small tasks off your desk as soon as you can. This can give a good feeling of satisfaction at having completed several tasks in one go.

3. Whatever the task or request, write it down! An A4 notepad and pen should accompany you whenever you leave your desk to go into the boss's office or anywhere else around the organisation. Write down messages, phone numbers, names, requests, enquiries – always in the same book. Don't rely on random scraps of paper or sticky notes for noting down your work: sticky notes are fine for random items such as inspirational notes to yourself or reminders to buy a newspaper on your way home – but don't use them for noting down work tasks. And don't have two or more notebooks on the go – keep everything in one book When you are back at your desk, transfer the vital information into your "to do" list.

4. Get a digital pen. As I've said, if you work for someone who reels out a number of tasks for you all in one breath and you find it hard to take it all in at one sitting, you might consider investing in a recording device: not necessarily so that they can dictate reams of letters for you, but to assist you with taking notes.

5. Check, double check and triple check. If you are unsure about something, ask. Make sure that you know what is being asked of you, so that you can get the task done, correctly and on time. Rushing into something with only half an idea of what's required will inevitably lose time and waste effort.

6. Use the "alert" function in your calendar to remind you to perform certain timely tasks. For example, if your boss has to leave by 2 pm to attend a meeting, make sure to set an alarm in your calendar for 12 pm to make

sure that he has the right papers (and travel details, map, parking details etc.) in his briefcase. You may have already done this earlier in the day, but the alert is your backup reminder system to ensure that you don't forget. Set a further reminder for 1:45 pm to remind him that he needs to be leaving in the next ten to fifteen minutes.

7. Take a regular break – get up, walk around, get a drink. Repeatedly and rapidly switching your brain from one task to another uses energy, so give yourself a few minutes at regular intervals to allow you to clear your head and combat any feelings of stress.

8. 'Eat the frog': if you have a horrible task that you really dislike but which has to be done on a regular basis (like filing), get it done and out of the way towards the beginning of your day. The reference to 'eat the frog' is from a common motivational story that "if you have to do something horrible (e.g. you have to eat a frog each day), do it first thing to get it over and done with, then move on to the next task. And if you have two horrible tasks to do – two frogs to eat – each day, eat the ugliest one first."

You can also look out for lists of handy tips on the internet, things which will help you to get more value out of the time in your day. You might find something like this, from the careers advice website www.TheMuse.com:

---

10 Productive Things You Can Do in Just a Minute

It's pretty hard to find a spare hour in the work day, but I bet you can find a minute here and there. Like when you are on hold or waiting for a meeting to start. That time can really add up so why not use those minutes for something useful? Here are ten things you can do next time you have one to spare.

1. identify one thing you can delegate

2. post an interesting article on LinkedIn

3. .download pocket and save a few articles you want to read later

4. download a productive app like card munch or do

5. delete an app that distracts you

6. send a thank you email to someone who has helped you

7. test all the pens on your desk and throw out the ones that don't work

8. organise your computer desktop

9. ask a co-worker you don't know very well out to lunch, and

10. prepare a list of questions to ask them about their role.

INVITE PEOPLE TO THE CIRCUS

9. NETWORKING WITH OTHER PAS / EAS

The Bill Poster-er: using your skills to network with other PAs / EAs

The role of a PA / EA can be incredibly isolating,

We live and breathe at our desks; our office walls are the boundaries of our working world. It is important that we are able to peer over the edge of the desk every now and then, to encounter the worlds of others in parallel roles from whom we can learn and who can learn from us. There are PAs, EAs, secretaries and other administrators out there who are experiencing similar frustrations, similar highs and lows, similar challenges and similar experiences.

Networking with other PAs and EAs allows you to reach out and connect with them, to share knowledge, expertise, learning, frustrations and delights. Share the wealth of your knowledge and expertise, not just with other administrators within your own organisation, but with others in the same field elsewhere.

You may well meet naysayers who claim that there is no worth in networking. However, more and more Executives are joining email discussion groups and/or LinkedIn groups, and sharing their knowledge and expertise. Most Executives regularly meet with the Executives, so if you want to know more about what you could get out of being in a network, ask your boss what they get from theirs!

Networking can be immensely useful for PAs and EAs. Sometimes, just knowing that there is someone else out there who has experienced something similar to what you might be going through, and who you could ask for help, advice or a listening ear, can be enough, without even having to call on them for their assistance. Being able to meet up with them on a semi-regular basis, or being able to reach them by phone or email, can make all the difference between being given an almost insurmountable task and completing it successfully, because you have drawn on the experience of someone else with the know-how.

There are several routes to networking – I'm going to recommend in particular using LinkedIn.com and meeting face-to-face with PAs and EAs.

Are YOU LinkedIn?

The most influential networking places for PAs / EAs is LinkedIn., and I always encourage everyone on my training courses to join it and actively take part in some form of networking on the site.

I'm a prolific networker, and since 2009 I've been the 'most connected PA on the planet', as one networking colleague calls me. On LinkedIn I'm connected at first level to over 22,000 people, and I have the largest network of any personal assistant, executive assistant, admin and trainer of PAs.

In addition, I created the 'PAs, EAs, VAs and Senior Administrators' group which currently has around 70,000 members. Networking has enabled me to entirely change my career, leading me to a 'real job' which includes me doing two things I would never have dreamed of before: collecting frequent flyer miles whilst working with some of the most amazing PAs in the world!

Of course, building an absolutely massive network isn't for everybody. I *do* realise that. But networking on any scale can have huge importance for you… it opens your mind to new possibilities by connecting and sharing with professionals in similar roles elsewhere.

Now, I'm ridiculously well connected, we know that. Please don't think thought you that if you join LinkedIn you have to try to emulate this. In fact, you don't have to connect with anyone at all if you don't want to. But one function of LinkedIn that you need to use is the 'Groups' facility: discussion forums exist on LinkedIn for thousands of topics and careers. **Joining a discussion group for PAs and EAs offers an enormous source of resources for developing in your role.**

Yes, you can of course choose to build a network of contacts all round the world, linking with ex college mates, former colleagues, your current colleagues, people who work in organisations you aspire to one day work in, etc. – these can all be incredibly helpful to your career. **I'd recommend at the very least that you connect with one super-connector such as myself.** Why? Because everything on LinkedIn works on a three level basis:

- your direct connections are your first level,
- the people they are connected to are your second level,
- and the people whom they are connected to are your third level.

When you conduct a search on the site for any individual (for example, if your Executive or Manager asks you to look up a particular candidate who has applied to your organisation for a job – or if you are searching to find an interim finance director, the reach of your search will be restricted to your three level network. If you only have a tiny network, this means that you will struggle to get any meaningful search results. For example, if you have only 10 connections at first level and they only have 10 connections each and those people have only 10 connections each, you will have an incredibly small and insignificant reach across the website (10 people plus their 100 connections, plus those 100's connections – making a total network of 1110). Whereas, having a larger network gives the potential of finding better – or more – results that suit your needs.

You could spend a lot of time building a large network on LinkedIn – or you can go through a shortcut route. By connecting with a 'super-connector' (that is, someone with a very large network), their first and second level connections will become your second and third level connections.

What does that equate to in numbers? Well, I have more than 22,000 first level and around 5 million second level connections – so, if you connect with me, that will give you an "instant" three level network of around 5 million people, with me as your first level connection and my 22,000+ as your second level. This means if you perform a search on the site, you will have a reach of around 5 million people from which to find results – before you even connect with anyone else.

If you'd like to connect with me on LinkedIn, you would be very welcome to. Details on this are in the Resources section at the back of this book.

How do you 'do' LinkedIn?

If you've never used the site before, go to www.linkedin.com and register for free. Create your own profile page – as detailed as you wish. At bare minimum, put your current role details.

From here, you can search for business people worldwide or just in your area or country, and send them invitations to connect with you. Click the icon directly to the left of the LinkedIn search bar at the top of the site in order to select the type of thing you wish to search for – a person, a company, a group, etc. Enter your search parameters in this box – or click the 'Advanced Search' button to the right in order to enter more detail to your search. And away you go!

I can recommend a few PA and EA related groups that I think you should join.

- PAs, EAs, VAs and Senior Admins – this is one of the groups that I created on LinkedIn. At latest count (August 2015) it has over 72,000 members.
- Executive Assistants to CEOs
- Executive Secretary
- PA Life.

Users on LinkedIn are permitted to join a maximum of 50 groups. This is a scary number for someone setting out on the site – do not attempt it! Just join a select few groups.

There are a few settings you might like to change, to suit you, particularly when starting out.

In every group you can change your settings, to determine when (if ever) you allow that group to send you email messages. These settings can be reached by clicking the small cog shaped icon at the right hand side of the group's name banner (once you have joined the group). The default setting is that a group can send you regular emails of the "best of" the day's messages. You can change this to weekly, or not at all, whichever you choose.

Whenever you interact in the group and send a message or a reply to someone else's message, you have the option of being emailed on any further replies from other users – you can change this to suit you for each and every discussion.

If you do choose to receive emails from the group, you might want to set up a filter in your email package so that messages from it go straight to an assigned 'LinkedIn' folder, rather than just staying in your main Inbox – this then means that you can choose when you go to read your various LinkedIn messages and they are not in the way of other emails.

When you join a group, any member of the group can post a question as a new discussion item – or respond to anyone else's discussion – and this means that any of the PA-related groups can be an absolute mine of information to help you in your role. For example: posting a question like "My boss has to go to Dubai next week for a conference, can anyone here recommend a good limo company to pick him up at the airport?" you will find that you'll generally receive a number of responses back, within a relatively short time.

Equally, you can (and should) jump into a discussion and participate. If you see a topic that interests you or a question which you believe you can answer, do so – just type into the 'comment' box below any discussion item. Share the wealth of your knowledge!

Face to face networking

Networking in person is a completely different matter. Communicating via the internet on a networking site can feel easy once you get used to the website. But meeting people in person and working out what to say to them, making small talk, creating relationships with new people? Ooooh, scary!

Hang on, though – you probably meet people in your role, don't you? Visitors who have come to meet with your boss? I'm sure you greet them and make a bit of small talk while they are waiting? (Hint: if you don't, then you should!)

If there isn't a ready-made network for you to join locally, you might consider setting up your own for PAs / EAs working in other organisations in your city or an internal network within your own organisation. You will undoubtedly have contact details for a lot of other PAs and EAs out there, from your communications with their offices on behalf of your Executive / Manager. Send out invitations to an afternoon or evening meeting where you can introduce yourselves, discuss training needs and perhaps offer to help each other.

Your network should aim to have a regular meeting to discuss continuing professional development (CPD) items in person, so that you can further yourselves in your careers. You will probably find it hard work to get PAs to attend these meetings – everyone will be 'too busy', or it will be 'too far', or it won't be seen as 'important enough' – but please keep prompting them to make time to attend. As soon as they have attended a meeting with other PAs, they will begin to see how useful it can be – especially when they start to put names to the faces of their peers from other organisations – and will be keen to attend again in the future. The best way for us all to become great in our jobs is to share our knowledge, to learn from each other, to develop each other's skills and to build on our knowledge collectively.

Effective Networking

Regardless of where you are – at the office, visiting a client, attending an event – networking is vital for your professional advancement. It is one of the best ways to make yourself known to others, while connecting with people who may be advantageous to your success at some point down the road.

Too often we are intimidated when thinking of meeting new people who are outside of our own "comfort" zone. Maybe we enter a room and realise we don't know a single person. Thus, we retreat to the food line, grab a few munchies, maybe wander aimlessly about or sit in a corner. At the opposite end of the spectrum, maybe we find that we are talking to the same people over and over, never venturing out beyond our own "group" to see who else might be worth meeting.

Yes, the art of networking is an acquired skill – but it is a skill that can be easily mastered with a little practice. The key to networking is to have interpersonal communication skills that are top notch. The trick is knowing how to start a conversation, keep it flowing, and end on a high note. Preparing in advance before attending the event will help to make your networking attempts much easier, while ensuring you have the greatest success.

What are you attending?

Make a short list of who will be at this event, the general purpose, is there anything you need to know before going (such as background information about the company, organization, or group), where it will be held, what time it starts, etc.

Why are you attending?

How will this benefit you personally? Professionally? Make a decision before you go as to what goal you would like to achieve – i.e., meet 3 people in the same industry as you are.

Who are you?

If you are going to interface with others, they are bound to ask about you. Have a prepared "blurb" to give about yourself. Be sure you mention how who you are relates to what the event is about. For example, if you are attending an organization event for your job, you would say something like "I'm Betty Smith and I have been with the company for 10 years now."

What will you say?

This is the one place at which "talk is not cheap." In fact, everything you say is a launching point for a potential future opportunity. Have some thoughts in your mind about local and national issues. If you find the conversation dwindling and all the small talk is done, resort to talking about the function, the facility, etc.

How well do you present yourself?

One of the keys to networking is to make others want to converse with you. Thus, being well spoken is a must. Before attending a function, try practicing starting a conversation on an interesting topic with which you are quite familiar. This can be anything from a best-selling novel, to a major event that a family member was involved in, to a unique project you are undertaking.

Once you arrive at the event, you'll want to make sure you mix and mingle effectively:

Shaking hands. Be sure to shake hands with people. It should be a professional handshake that you would use when greeting a customer or client. Not too firm, yet firm enough to make a connection.

Actively listening. When you speak with someone, be sure to maintain good eye contact. Listen to what they say and ask relevant questions. Focus on how they express themselves, and how they respond to what you are saying.

Be helpful. If you are comfortable circulating about and talking to anyone and everyone, try paying attention to people that seem as if they have lost their way. Introduce yourself and ask if you can help them find something, someone, or answer any questions. Imagine you are an old pro at this and make this other person feel welcome.

Volunteer. If the event has opportunities for which you can volunteer either before or during, by all means raise your hand. This will give you instant exposure to the greatest number of people. Plus, it is also an excellent way to improve and enhance your skill set.

Have a card. Granted, secretarial and administrative professionals don't generally have a business card. However, that doesn't mean you can't create one for yourself. Many of the major office supply stores now sell full-colour, pre-cut business card sheets that you can simply run through a laser printer. Include your name, a title (e.g., Administrative Professional, Secretary Extraordinaire, etc.), phone number, email address, web site (if you have one), and any other tidbits about yourself. Feel free to use both sides of the card. In fact, the back side is ideal to put a small bulleted list of your experience – somewhat like a mini-resume (and very mini resume obviously). For example, "15 Years Administrative Experience" or "Associates Degree in Business from USC," etc.

Gather cards. If you meet someone and feel there might be a connection, ask for his/her card. If he/she doesn't have a card, have some small sheets of paper readily available and a pen so that you can get the desired information. Never assume the company, organization, or group is going to provide a list of attendees. While this was a popular thing to do in years gone by, most events no longer offer this for a variety of reasons: time involved to organise and assemble, protecting the privacy of attendees, giving confidential information to potential competitors in attendance, etc.

Follow up. Once the event is over, be sure to make contact with those people you've met. This contact can be anything from just a quick hand written note that says, "it was nice to meet you" to an email that highlights some of the things you have in common and any opportunities that may be present to work together again. Try and find a reason to keep your communication with selected people going forward. This doesn't mean you have to become best buddies – but instead professionals who share some common interests.

There are an enormous number of PA and EA related networks worldwide. Any listing of these would no doubt be out of date as soon as a book is printed, so to check the most up-to-date details on the ASSOCIATIONS page at www.executivesecretary.com. This is the website of 'Executive Secretary', a global magazine for PAs and EAs, and an excellent source of resources and training articles, written by influential people and trainers in administration. The website also includes an extensive diary of PA / EA training events taking place all over the world.

"PLEASE DON'T LET ME DROP THEM, PLEASE DON'T LET ME DROP THEM...."

10. JUGGLING PRIORITIES AND SCHEDULING

The Juggler can shuffle priorities and schedules

Every PA / EA will develop their own system of prioritising their workload over the course of time. There are many books out there on scheduling work – or you can talk with your colleagues in the admin team to find out what they do, learn from your boss, discuss with your mentor, find out what works for other PAs in your network – and then pick and choose from these to develop your own systems and methods.

The main thing you should make sure to include in your system is to TALK with your Executive(s) on a regular basis to ensure that you are meeting their priorities, not just the ones you perceive that they need.

Here are a collection of methods for helping you to plan, prioritise, and schedule your workload, whilst remaining flexible and adaptable enough to take on new priorities as they appear.

5 Key principles for planning a week effectively:

1. Keep an up to date list of everything that you currently have to do (your Action List)

2. Find 30 minutes at the same time every week to plan your week – identifying priorities.

3. Use your diary to book time to complete activities and also book time for admin activities (e.g. reviewing inbox, filing, managing emails or meeting preparation, planning)

4. Review your Diary and your Action List every morning to establish your priorities for the day.

   Write them on one page of paper and keep it on your desk. If you do nothing else today – do these and you will have had a good day.

5. Review. As priorities change, be prepared to adapt and be flexible

Is the Pressure Getting to You?

Time has become the number one concern for most people.

There is never enough time to accomplish everything, let alone the priorities. If you have a continual, unrelenting stream of tasks, there are a few steps you can take to maximise your effectiveness and make time work for you.

Put it in writing. The simple act of putting words on a page (either on paper or your computer screen) allows you to see exactly what it is you have to do, and to prioritise the tasks shown.

Create your own due dates. You know whether or not you are a good manager of your own time. Since most of us are not, include realistic due dates with each listed task, based upon your work habits.

For example, if you know that Project X is due next Monday and it will take you 3 days to complete, set a cushioned due date of 5 days. This will ensure that you start early enough, and allow for any "unforeseen" circumstances.

Do something for you! Commit that you will include one task on your "to do" list that is just for you. Maybe your work area could use a little sprucing up, so straight after lunch do a 10 minute tidy round. Or get up out of your chair during the mid-afternoon slump and take the walk you keep saying you should be taking. Take that bonus or raise and spend it on yourself.

Don't procrastinate. We always push off the toughest task to handle last, when, in fact, we should be doing just the opposite.

Completing that tough task first provides a tremendous relief and can actually motivate us to a higher level, so that we work more efficiently and effectively on those tasks that aren't so hard.

Minimise distractions. Just say no. There are only so many hours in a day and if it cannot be done, it cannot be done.

Top Tips to Scheduling Tasks

- Schedule them: one "BHT" (Big Horrible Task) each morning. "Eat the frog / bag of worms!"

- Touch a piece of paper only once.. or bite a bit off – you'll have to do it before you finish eating it!

- Take a treat with a dull task – "I'll finish this, then have a cup of tea."

- For big tasks – break things down into smaller tasks and take on one piece per day. You can't eat an elephant whole. One foot at a time.

- An important task can become urgent if you keep putting it off every day.

- Try to tackle at least 5 important tasks daily – including simple tasks like phone calls that are essential for moving a project along.

- Differentiate between "simultaneous" and "sequential" tasks – there are some things that you can do while other tasks are taking place, but other things that you can't do until something else has been done first – so line these tasks up in you "to do" lists appropriately. There's no point starting on part (b) or (c) of a task if both of these rely on you having completed part (a) first and you haven't done that part of the work yet…

Remembering not to aim for perfection because good enough will do –

It pays to manage your time well because it is a fact that managing your time well makes you successful. Good time management can help to level the playing field between natural winners and the rest of mankind.

A good strategy is to remind yourself that for busy office professionals, doing things perfectly is less valuable to your organisation than doing things adequately.

Doing things adequately will allow sufficient time in your time budget to stay on top of important projects and make important deadlines.

It is tempting to re-word that paragraph in your email one more time before hitting the send button, because you love to write and want to get it word perfect, but "good enough" will do.

You can actually waste a lot of valuable time, that could be spent on other tasks or projects, in trying to get a piece of work to the level of perfection. Make sure that it is adequate and correct, and does what is required – and then MOVE ON!

It also helps to know what you are worth!

Calculate how much your time is worth, and record how you spend your time.

Knowing the value of your time should help you to allocate your time effectively.

For example, if you are paid a certain amount per hour, think of that amount when you spend an hour on a task: does this particular task warrant that amount of money being spent on it, in comparison with your other tasks and duties for which you are being paid the same amount of money for an hour? If it doesn't, spend less time on it.

< PARP! PARP! >

11. STOP CLOWNING AROUND AND WORK 'SMARTER'

Don't be a clown: plan to work SMARTER not harder.

Give yourself a break when you are doing your planning. Don't plan unrealistically – and make sure you plan adequately for whatever you need to do. Not making plans won't get you by – but making the wrong kind of plans is equally bad. So, when you are planning, a good thing for you to do is to always set yourself targets and goals that follow the **SMARTER** acronym: I hate acronyms usually, but for this chapter I will make one exception, as I believe it is actually really useful...

The idea of Managing by Objectives stems from Peter Drucker's 1954 book "The Practice of Management". In the ensuring years the SMART acronym came into common usage within goal setting and performance appraisal or management environments, and was later extended into SMARTER.

The acronym provides the basis for creating objectives for managing performance or developmental purposes.

Variations of words commonly used in SMART as an acronym.

S	Specific, Stimulating, Sincere, Simple, Stretching, Succinct, Straight-forward, Self-owned, Self-managed, Self-controlled, Significant, Strategic, Sensible
M	Measurable, Motivating, Manageable, Meaningful, Magical, Magnetic, Maintainable, Mapped-to-goals
A	Achievable, Assignable Appropriate, Audacious, Actionable, Attainable, Ambitious, Aspirational, Accepted-or-acceptable, Aligned, Accountable, Agreed, Adapted, As-if-now, Adjustable, Adaptable
R	Realistic, Relevant, Results Orientated, Resources are adequate, Resourced, Rewarding, Recorded, Reviewable, Robust, Relevant to a mission
T	Timely, Time-bound, Time-limited, Time-driven, Time-constrained, Time-constricted, Time-related, Time-phased, Time-sensitive, Time-

	specific, Time-stamped, Time-lined, Tangible, Trackable, Traceable, Timed, Timely, Toward what you want, Team-Building
E	Evaluate, Empowering, Extending, Exciting, Encompassing, Engaging, Energising, Ethical, Enjoyable
R	Review, Rewarding, Record, Realistic, Relevant, Resourced, Research Based

One of the key advantages in using SMARTER in the agreeing and setting of personal development goals, is that it helps to recognise the importance of the engagement of the individual. The more motivated they are by the development objective the better they appear to perform, often putting extra time into self-development activity.

My interpretation of the SMARTER acronym which I use for my work is:

S pecific

M easurable

A chievable

R ealistic

T imely

E valuate

R eview

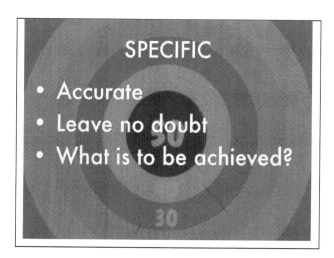

MEASURABLE

- When will the project be complete?
- How will I know?

ACHIEVABLE

- Make the project as small as possible
- Easier to manage small projects
- Harder to manage large projects
- The smaller the elephant, the easier is it to eat

REALISTIC

- Make it easy
- If complicated, likely to have problems
- Easy = under budget
- Easy = good quality
- Easy = on time

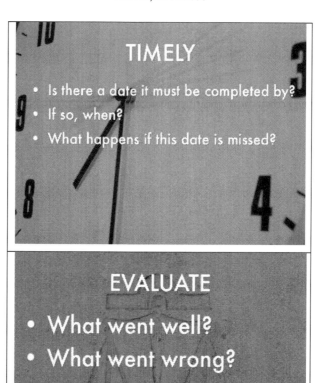

TIMELY
- Is there a date it must be completed by?
- If so, when?
- What happens if this date is missed?

EVALUATE
- What went well?
- What went wrong?

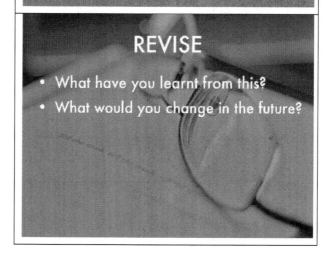

REVISE
- What have you learnt from this?
- What would you change in the future?

Decide on your version of the SMARTER acronym, with words that are appropriate to your company or your industry.

Then decide how you are going to start using it as the basis of how you approach ALL of your work.

Work SMARTER, not harder. It's a no-brainer.

HUMAN JENGA... REMOVE ONE AND THE WHOLE TOWER MIGHT FALL

12. GETTING ALONG WITH OTHERS

The Human Pyramid: from the bottom of the organisation to the top, you have to be able to get along with people on all levels

It is wonderful if you make friends with anyone at work. We don't go there, as PAs and EAs, with "making friends" as a purpose of our being there, of course. We go there to support our boss and to interact in a friendly manner with everyone. But if it does come to it that you make some personal friends at work, it is a nice bonus.

Indeed, according to the Gallup Organization, people who have a best friend at work are seven times more likely to be engaged in their jobs. And it doesn't have to be a best friend: Gallup found that people who simply had a good friend in the workplace are more likely to be satisfied.

What makes a good working relationship?

- Trust – This is the foundation of every good relationship. When you trust your team and colleagues, you form a powerful bond that helps you work and communicate more effectively. If you trust the people you work with, you can be open and honest in your thoughts and actions, and you don't have to waste time and energy "watching your back."
- Mutual Respect – When you respect the people that you work with, you value their input and ideas, and they value yours. Working together, you can develop solutions based on your collective insight, wisdom and creativity.
- Mindfulness – This means taking responsibility for your words and actions. Those who are mindful are careful and attend to what they say, and they don't let their own negative emotions impact the people around them.
- Welcoming Diversity – People with good relationships not only accept diverse people and opinions, but they welcome them. For instance, when your friends and colleagues offer different opinions from yours, you take the time to consider what they have to say, and factor their insights into your decision-making.

- Open Communication – We communicate all day, whether we're sending emails and IMs, or meeting face-to-face. The better and more effectively you communicate with those around you, the richer your relationships will be. All good relationships depend on open, honest communication.

Building better relationships

However, let's look at that "friendly manner with everyone"... because it can be very hard to smile and be polite with someone who is difficult.

One of your skills to develop then is the ability to deal professionally with everyone you come into contact with – whether the lowest member of staff up to the highest, and everyone in between – together with customers, board directors, suppliers. In short, everyone you come into contact with.

Some steps you might use to build better working relationships with your colleagues could include:

- Develop Your People Skills: Good relationships start with good people skills. Take our How Good Are Your People Skills? quiz to find out how well you score with "soft skills" such as collaboration, communication and conflict resolution. This self-test will point you to tools that will help you deal with any weaknesses that you have.
- Identify Your Relationship Needs: Look at your own relationship needs. Do you know what you need from others? And do you know what they need from you? Understanding these needs can be instrumental in building better relationships.
- Schedule Time to Build Relationships: Devote a portion of your day toward relationship building, even if it is just 20 minutes, perhaps broken up into five-minute segments. For example, you could pop into someone's office during lunch, reply to people's postings on Twitter or LinkedIn , or ask a colleague out for a quick cup of coffee. These little interactions help build the foundation of a good relationship, especially if they are face-to-face.
- Focus on Your EI: Also, spend time developing your emotional intelligence (EI). Among other things, this is your ability to recognise your own emotions, and clearly understand what they are telling you. High EI also helps you to understand the emotions and needs of others.
- Appreciate Others: Show your appreciation whenever someone helps you. Everyone, from your boss to the office cleaner, wants to feel that their work is appreciated. So, genuinely compliment the people around you when they do something well. This will open the door to great work relationships.

- Be Positive: Focus on being positive. Positivity is attractive and contagious, and it will help strengthen your relationships with your colleagues. No one wants to be around someone who's negative all the time.
- Manage Your Boundaries: Make sure that you set and manage boundaries properly – all of us want to have friends at work, but, occasionally, a friendship can start to impact our jobs, especially when a friend or colleague begins to monopolise our time. If this happens, it is important that you are assertive about your boundaries, and that you know how much time you can devote during the work day for social interactions.
- Avoid Gossiping: Don't gossip – office politics and "gossip" are major relationship killers at work. If you are experiencing conflict with someone in your group, talk to them directly about the problem. Gossiping about the situation with other colleagues will only exacerbate the situation, and will cause mistrust and animosity between you.
- Listen Actively: Practice active listening when you talk to your customers and colleagues. People respond to those who truly listen to what they have to say. Focus on listening more than you talk, and you'll quickly become known as someone who can be trusted.

Difficult relationships

It is, of course, inevitable that at some point in our careers we are going to come up against some characters with whom we have difficulty getting along. Sometimes it is a personality clash, sometimes it is someone's mannerisms that get your back up. Other times it is what they say or how they say it.

People's actions – or inaction – can cause difficulty – and feelings of unfairness or favouritism by certain bosses towards certain employees can often cause rumour and speculation throughout the workplace. We meet people all the time who we just don't feel an affinity with.

But if or when the working relationship with them becomes toxic – when they are having a negative impact on you or your work, or when you are worrying how to deal with some of their actions – then you really do have to try to find a solution. For the sake of your work, it is essential you maintain a professional relationship with them.

When this happens, make an effort to get to know the person. It is likely that they know full well that the two of you aren't on the best terms, so make the first move to improve the relationship by engaging them in a genuine conversation, or by inviting them out to lunch.

While you are talking, try not to be too guarded. Ask them about their background, interests and past successes. Instead of putting energy into your differences, focus on finding things that you have in common.

Just remember – not all relationships will be great; but you can make sure that they are, at least, workable!

Below is a light-hearted look at spotting and recognising some of the major "bad news" colleagues you might come across in your career.

Identifying when you have 'toxic colleagues'

I met a snake at one of my recent training events: a really venomous, dangerous snake. I'm not sure of her name, or where she was from. From our conversation I ascertained that she is in her mid-fifties and deeply unhappy with her life. For now, let's just call her Miss Snake.

Like most of the people attending my courses, Miss Snake works in a school. She attended a session that I gave, and later that day she tried to pick a verbal fight with me about some issues she had with my subject matter.

Why do I call her a snake? Quite simply because to anybody else in the room who might been watching, they would probably have thought that she was having a lovely conversation with me: she was smiling sweetly throughout, regardless of the venomous words coming out of her mouth.

I have no problem with anybody who attends one of my courses or seminars in giving me some feedback. I'm quite happy to take on board criticisms or comments that I may have said something that wasn't clear, or questions about where I got my information from.

This woman, Miss Snake, did not offer criticisms or comments, or seek clarification. She didn't speak to me as if I was a peer – she spoke to me as if I was something unpleasant that she had trodden in. She tried to break me down by being downright unpleasant, rude, nasty, and by continually speaking over me and not allowing me to answer.

All the while, she smiled sweetly, her eyes lighting on other people across the room and flashing her teeth at them. To all intents and purposes she looked like she was telling me how much she enjoyed my seminar.

Her criticisms centred around one major point of my seminar, regarding future planning. I am very passionate about PAs, as I believe we have some of the greatest skills in the workplace. I'm very passionate that we should receive excellent training opportunities and be able to make the very best of ourselves.

I'm also passionate that we should have a great work / home life balance – and that, whatever our aspirations may be, we have a chance of reaching them. I don't believe that every PA should be constantly reaching for the stars in everything they do, all day, every day, or that we should all try to be the most ambitious person ever.

However, I do believe that we all need to have an idea of where we are going, if for nothing else than to have an idea of what we might like to do when, one day, we hang up our audio typing headphones, put away our pencils and stop organising the boss's diary – in other words, what we might do in our retirement.

Miss Snake was clearly unhappy that I have mentioned this within my seminar that afternoon. She criticised my emphasis on the importance of PAs having some sort of a plan to further their career. She said "that's rubbish about the PA having a career plan, PAs don't have a career OR a plan. I for one don't care where I am in 10 or 15 years' time. In fact, I hope I'm dead in 15 years' time."

I was astounded. This came from the mouth of a woman who works in a school, with children who could be easily influenced by her words, her attitude, her actions. I felt that there was nothing I could say to this woman other than to ask her, with a look of innocence, "Then what are you doing at a CPD event? What on earth are you trying to develop?" She was unable to give me an answer, and I extracted myself from my conversation with this woman as soon as I could.

Sometimes there is no point in trying to win an argument just for the sake of winning an argument. I was not going to win against a woman with such a downbeat attitude towards life, who frankly didn't care if she was dead in a few years' time. I don't want to spend my time talking to someone like that. I want to work with the living – Miss Snake seemed already emotionally dead, as far as her career and her life were concerned.

I went away deeply troubled by my conversation with this woman. To think that someone might have so little to look forward to felt depressing and disturbing. I wish her well. Mostly, I hope that I will never have that attitude myself. Nor that anyone I know will have it – and that they will instead look forward to living fully and enjoying themselves.

Whether you have or haven't yet had the 'pleasure' of working with any of the people portrayed on the next couple of pages, have a think about how you might interact with them better in future…

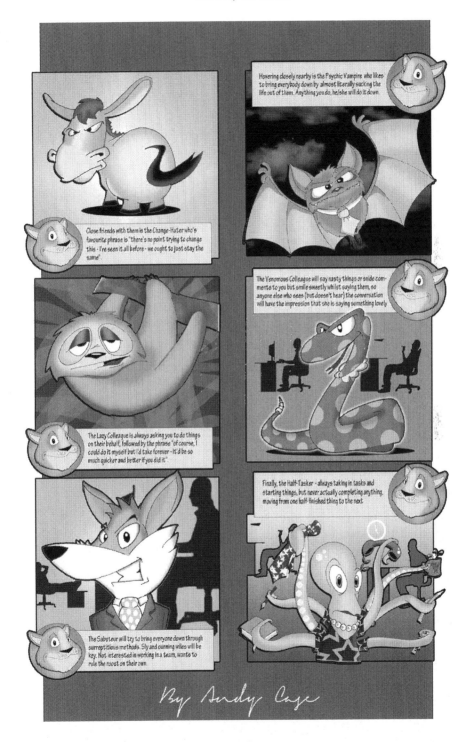

By Andy Case

"IT TAKES A WHILE TO TRAIN AN ELEPHANT, YOU KNOW – THERE ARE A LOT OF STEPS"

13. HANDLING TASKS WITH PROJECT MANAGEMENT TOOLS

The Elephant Trainer takes on the big tasks – project management

So, you started out as a PA / EA a few years ago, and now you are maybe mid-career. How has your career evolved so far? Have you done regular CPD to ensure that you are moving forward, always embracing new technologies, new methods of working, new ideas and new strategies?

Some of the tools you may find you need, as your PA / EA career progresses, are productivity tools – skills and methods that can help you with managing projects. Many PAs dread being offered 'project management' as they feel that this is something outside of their realm of possibility.

To be honest though, most of us in the PA / EA world handle projects all of the time, we just don't think of it in terms of actually being 'project management'.

The first step towards good project management is recognising that you already have many of the skills required to be a successful project manager: good organisational skills, planning skills, working to deadline, prioritising, scheduling, handling pressurised situations, and ensuring that everything gets done at the right time at the right place and to budget. All of these are vital skills in project management.

Another important thing with project management is to break the project down into much smaller, more manageable parts: then look at the resources available to you (staffing, time, budget, equipment, skills within the workforce) and then start matching skills / staff to parts of the project.

Another vital tactic is to ensure that each part of the project is planned SMARTER – make sure you know what you are dealing with and it will all slot into place.

You may find it helpful to use a mind-map to plan this out – there are a number of free mind-mapping software packages which can help with this – or just start with a big sheet of paper!

A Gantt chart (deadline planning chart) is really useful for keeping track of deadlines and timescales – again, there are plenty of easy-to-use free software packages out there, or you could just use Excel…

If you haven't used mind-maps or Gantt charts before, here's some information on them:

Mind-mapping

A mind map is a diagram used to visually outline information, often created around a single word or text, to which associated ideas, words and concepts are added. Mind maps are considered to be a type of spider diagram. A similar concept in the 1970s was "idea sun bursting". This technique can be used to determine how many tasks will evolve from the main task or project and which to complete first.

To create a basic mind-map, write the project name (or the aim of whatever you are trying to achieve) in the centre of the page and draw lines pointing to each task within it. Then separate those out into sub-tasks, highlighting the fine detail associated with each aspect of the project.

This helps you to see those items which must be completed sequentially or can be completed simultaneously so you can time your projects and tasks adequately to meet deadlines.

A real-life example might be looking at the Monthly Presentation which your manager has to make to the Board of Directors: Start by putting the aim in the middle of your paper.

Around the aim, add some lines to represent the various main strands which will go towards creating the presentation:

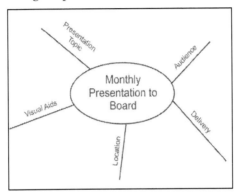

Then expand the main strands further into subdivisions:

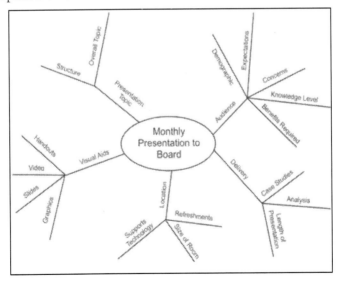

More and more sub-strands are added as the project builds....

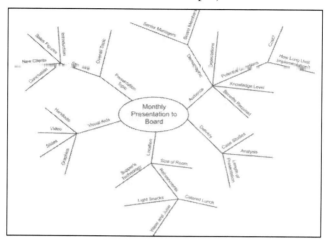

Gantt Chart

A Gantt chart is a type of bar chart, developed by Henry Gantt in the 1910s, that illustrates a project schedule.

Gantt charts illustrate the start and finish dates of the terminal elements and summary elements of a project. Terminal elements and summary elements comprise the work breakdown structure of the project.

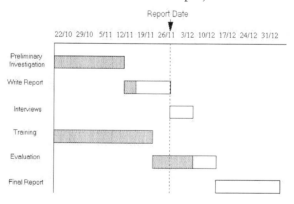

Some Gantt charts also show the dependency (i.e. precedence network) relationships between activities.

Gantt charts can be used to show current schedule status using percent-complete shadings and a vertical "TODAY" line as shown overleaf.

Automated Gantt charts store more information about tasks, such as the individuals assigned to specific tasks, and notes about the procedures. They also offer the benefit of being easy to change, which is helpful.

Charts may be adjusted frequently to reflect the actual status of project tasks as, almost inevitably, they diverge from the original plan.

Use your mind-map to help you generate your Gantt chart. Take the items listed in each strand and add them into your chart, with anticipated timings.

Some considerations:

Sometimes Gantt charts are drawn with additional details: e.g. resources or skill level needed or person responsible.

Beware of identifying reviews or approvals as events unless they really will take place at a specific time, such as a meeting – as they can often take days or weeks.

The process of constructing the Gantt chart forces group members to think clearly about what must be done to accomplish their goal. Keeping the chart updated as the project proceeds helps manage the project and head off schedule problems.

It can be useful to indicate any critical points with bold or coloured outlines of the bars.

Both Mind-Mapping and Gantt charts are two fantastically useful tools to assist you with handling projects. Both can be created on paper – or by using the drawing functions in Word or by creating a table in Excel – or by using a specially designed package. It is well worth searching on the internet for "free mind-map software" or "free Gantt chart software" , and downloading and trialling something before you decide whether or not your company should be investing in anything more high powered – quite often, a free package will do everything you need it to and more!

"YOU WANT IT BY *WHEN*?
WHAT DO YOU THINK I AM, A MAGICIAN ?"

14. SOLVING PROBLEMS – JUST LIKE MAGIC!

The Magician: producing magical results to problems at the drop of a hat

As time goes by, you will find that your Executives are relying on you more and more as a helpful resource, a problem solver and an information source.

In order to meet these requirements, the up-and-coming PA / EA needs an adequate toolkit, full of things that help you fulfil the needs of your job.

Like project management, the mere idea of having to solve problems and make important decisions can instill fear or at least feel uncomfortable for the PA / EA who isn't used to having the responsibility for these.

Sometimes, some of the major problems we face require solving in different and innovative ways to produce the magical results that our Executives are expecting. In order to do this, here are a range of problem solving and decision making tools which can help you to do the "impossible".

Problem-solving often involves decision-making, and decision-making is especially important for management and leadership. There are processes and techniques to improve decision-making and the quality of decisions. Decision-making is more natural to certain personalities, so these people should focus more on improving the quality of their decisions. People who are less natural decision-makers are often able to make quality assessments, but then need to be more decisive in acting upon the assessments made.

Good decision-making requires a mixture of skills: creative development and identification of options, clarity of judgement, firmness of decision, and effective implementation. For group problem-solving and decision-making, or when a consensus is required, workshops help, within which you can incorporate these tools and process as appropriate.

Problem-solving and decision-making are closely linked, and each requires creativity in identifying and developing options. Once again, we already have a huge number of skills at our disposal.

Whichever one you choose to use to help you select the best option, make sure you can explain your reasonings for your decision to those involved, and follow up to ensure proper and effective implementation.

Brainstorming process:

Simply, this is a process which involves noting down any ideas at random – then going over them to extract themes, link items together, and create pathways from one item to another.

It can be used to.

Define and agree the objective.

Brainstorm ideas and suggestions having agreed a time limit.

Categorise/condense/combine/refine.

Assess/analyse effects or results.

Prioritise options/rank list as appropriate.

Agree action and timescale.

Control and monitor follow-up.

In a group situation, this needs to be controlled – I'd suggest 10 to 15 minute "all ideas thrown into the ring" approach, with none being discussed as right or wrong in the first instance.

After the allotted time, then start looking for themes or groupings in the ideas. Then cross out impossibilities. Then prioritise the rest.

SWOT and PESTEL Analysis:

Both techniques examine as issue from various angles, and can be immensely helpful in decision-making and problem-solving.

SWOT analysis helps assess the strength of a company, a business proposition or idea (by its internal Strengths and Weaknesses, and external Opportunities and Threats).

PESTEL analysis helps to assess the potential and suitability of a market (via Political, Economic, Social, Technological, Environmental and Legal factors).

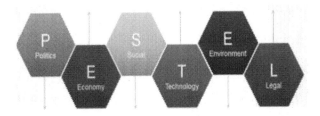

There are countless website which will assist you in using either of these techniques.

Pros and cons method

Pro means 'for', and con means 'against'. In other words, advantages and disadvantages.

This method also applies to all sorts of problem-solving where issues and implications need to be understood and a decision has to be made.

Some decisions are a simple matter of whether to make a change or not, such as moving, taking a new job, or buying something, selling something, replacing something, etc. Other decisions involve number of options, and are concerned more with how to do something, involving a number of choices. Use the brainstorming process to identify and develop options for decision-making and problem-solving.

- First you will need a separate sheet for each identified option.

- On each sheet write clearly the option concerned, and then beneath it the headings 'pros' and 'cons' (or 'advantages' and disadvantages', or simply 'for' and 'against'). Many decisions simply involve the choice of whether to go ahead or not, to change or not; in these cases you need only one sheet.

- Then write down as many effects and implications of the particular option that you (and others if appropriate) can think of, placing each in the relevant column.

- If helpful 'weight' each factor, by giving it a score out of three or five points (e.g., 5 being extremely significant, and 1 being of minor significance).

- When you have listed all the points you can think of for the option concerned compare the number or total score of the items/effects/factors between the two columns.

- This will provide a reflection and indication as to the overall attractiveness and benefit of the option concerned. If you have scored each item you will actually be able to arrive at a total score, being the difference between the pros and cons column totals. The bigger the difference between the total pros and total cons then the more attractive the option is.

- If you have a number of options and have complete a pros and cons sheet for each option, compare the attractiveness – points difference between pros and cons – for each option. The biggest positive difference between pros and cons is the most attractive option. Note: If you don't like the answer that the decision-making sheet(s) reflect back to you, it means you haven't included all the cons – especially the emotional ones, or you haven't scored the factors consistently, so re-visit the sheet(s) concerned.

- You will find that writing things down in this way will help you to see things more clearly, become more objective and detached, which will help you to make clearer decisions.

This example weighs the pros and cons of buying a new car to replace an old car – and with 6 pros scoring 20, against 5 cons scoring 16, the "best" result is deemed to be buying a new car.

Should I replace my old car with a new one?			
pros (for - advantages)	score	cons (against - disadvantages)	score
better comfort	3	cost outlay will mean making sacrifices	5
lower fuel costs	3	higher insurance	3
lower servicing costs	4	time and hassle to choose and buy it	2
better for family use	3	disposal or sale of old car	2
better reliability	5	big decisions like this scare and upset me	4
it'll be a load off my mind	2		
total 6 pros	20	total 5 cons	16

The weighted pros and cons are purely examples – they are not in any way suggestions of how you should make such a decision. Each person's decision-making criteria depend on their own personal situations and preferences.

Your criteria and weighting will change according to time, situation, and probably your mood too. Use whatever scoring method you want to. The example shows low scores but you can score each item up to 10, or 20 or 100 – whatever makes sense to you personally. Or you can use an 'A/B/C' or three-star scoring method, whatever works for you.

Paired Comparison

Compose a table that pits each option directly against each other option, cage-match-style, and weighting each for relative importance. A fast and bloodless way to plough through what would otherwise be a huge mess to evaluate. Useful for weighing up the relative importance of different options.

		Compared to			
	Asset A	Asset B	Asset C	Asset D	Total
Asset A		3	2	3	8
Asset B	1		3	2	6
Asset C	2	1		1	4
Asset D	1	2	3		6

(Asset — row label)

It is particularly helpful where priorities aren't clear, where the options are completely different, where evaluation criteria are subjective, or where they are competing in importance. The tool provides a framework for comparing each option against all others, and helps to show the difference in importance between factors.

Pareto Analysis

Often better known as "The 80/20 Rule," Pareto helps you locate where you can derive the greatest benefit by expending the least relative effort (or cost or resources or what have you).

Once you learn about the 80/20 rule, you start seeing instances of it everywhere. Identify and list problems and their causes. Then score each problem and group them together by their cause. Then add up the score for each group.

Finally, work on finding a solution to the cause of the problems in group with the highest score. Pareto Analysis not only shows you the most important problem to solve, it also gives you a score showing how severe the problem is.

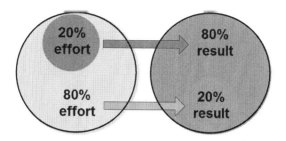

Grid Analysis

Evaluate a larger set of options based on numerous criteria, then weight the importance of each criterion to derive the best choice. Given the possibilities of some complex arithmetic, this technique can benefit from using Excel. This example looks at buying computer equipment from four different suppliers, gauging each supplier against five different factors. For the first "round" of the analysis, you award a score against each supplier for each factor.

Factors:	Cost	Quality	Location	Reliability	Payment Options	Total
Weights:						
Supplier 1	1	0	0	1	3	
Supplier 2	0	3	2	2	1	
Supplier 3	2	2	1	3	0	
Supplier 4	2	3	3	3	0	

Then, the five factors are put in order of importance (weighted 5 for most important down to 1 for least important), and their columns multiplied by the weighting. This yields the following result:

Factors:	Cost	Quality	Location	Reliability	Payment Options	Total
Weights:	4	5	1	2	3	
Supplier 1	4	0	0	2	9	15
Supplier 2	0	15	2	4	3	24
Supplier 3	8	10	1	6	0	25
Supplier 4	8	15	3	6	0	32

The "winning" supplier in this case, comes in as Supplier 4, with the highest score overall. Suppliers 2 and 3, which vied for equal second place in the first round of analysis, are ordered third and second respectively once the weighting of the factors has been multiplied in.

Decision Trees

Build a set of "what-ifs" based on a tree of possible options, assigning the estimated value, cost, or savings associated with each choice. This method is good for looking at all the possible options.

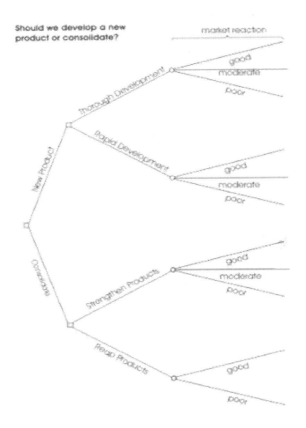

Six Thinking Hats - © Edward de Bono 1985
http://www.debonogroup.com/six_thinking_hats.php

A method for seeing an issue from all perspectives by forcing yourself (or more often your team) to—one at a time—adopt different "thinking hats" that reflect opposing and orthogonal points of view.

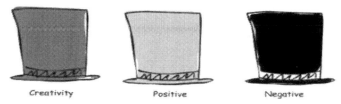

| Creativity | Positive | Negative |

- White Hat: focus on the data available. Look at the information you have, and see what you can learn from it. Look for gaps in your knowledge, and either try to fill them or take account of them. Analyse past trends, and try to extrapolate from historical data.
- Red Hat: look at problems using intuition, gut reaction, and emotion. Also try to think how other people will react emotionally. Try to understand the responses of people who do not fully know your reasoning.
- Black Hat: look at all the bad points of the decision. Look at it cautiously and defensively. Try to see why it might not work. This is important because it highlights the weak points in a plan. It allows you to eliminate them, alter them, or prepare contingency plans to counter them. This helps to make your plans 'tougher' and more resilient. It can also help you to spot fatal flaws and risks before you embark on a course of action. Black Hat thinking is one of the real benefits of this technique, as many successful people get so used to thinking positively that often they cannot see problems in advance. This leaves them under-prepared for difficulties.
- Yellow Hat: think positively. It is the optimistic viewpoint that helps you to see all the benefits of the decision and the value in it. Yellow Hat thinking helps you to keep going when everything looks gloomy and difficult.
- Green Hat: creativity. This is where you can develop creative solutions to a problem. It is a freewheeling way of thinking, in which there is little criticism of ideas. A whole range of creativity tools can help you here.
- Blue Hat: process control. This is the hat worn by people chairing meetings. When running into difficulties because ideas are running dry, they may direct activity into Green Hat thinking. When contingency plans are needed, they will ask for Black Hat thinking, etc.

PMI

List all the **pluses, minuses, and implications** behind any decision ("I" could also refer to **interesting or intriguing** data points). Then assign a + or − numerical value to each based on the positive or negative impact. Tally up the columns, and your better option emerges. This method takes the emotion and guesswork out of complex decisions, with the side benefit of forcing a brain dump. Easy to do in Excel (or on paper).

What's good +	What's bad -	What's interesting ?

Force Field

Identify all the forces for and against a theoretical change, weighted for amount of force exerted by each "side." Useful for touchy political decisions or any time a well-established more is going to be challenged, and might help in mitigating risk and knowing where best to allocate your resources and influence.

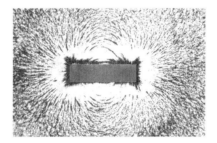

Cost/Benefit Analysis

This is an evergreen you've probably used a dozen or more times; estimate the costs and the benefits and decide if the task or project is worth the hassle. As ever, be sure to account for all the costs of a change, including the small stuff.

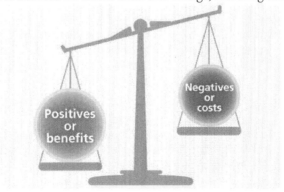

"GIVE ME STRENGTH...."

15. COPING WITH THE STRESSES AND STRAINS

The Strong Woman / Strong Man: coping with the stresses and strains of supporting the Circus

Is the pressure of your role getting to you?

Time (or, more pertinently, not having enough of it) is often named as the number one concern for most people in the workplace. There is never enough time to accomplish everything, let alone managing all of the various priorities that PAs have to deal with.

If in your role you have a continual, unrelenting stream of tasks, it can feel very daunting, as there seems to be no light at the end of the tunnel.

Here are some of my tips to help maximise your effectiveness and make time work for you., whilst allowing yourself some time and space to de-stress a little.

- **Do something for you!** Commit to including one task on your to-do list that is for you. Make a stop-off whilst on the way to the photocopier or elsewhere in the building, to say "hello" to another colleague in their office and ask them to lunch. Maybe your work area could use a little sprucing up, so straight after lunch do a 10 minute tidy round. Get up out of your chair during the mid-afternoon slump and take the walk you keep saying you should be taking. Book a telephone call with your mentor to discuss your latest project. Or take a few minutes to log into LinkedIn, read some of the discussions in a PA / EA group, and answer someone's query.

- **Don't procrastinate.** We always put off the toughest task until last, when, in fact, we should be doing just the opposite. Completing that tough task first provides a tremendous relief and can actually motivate us to a higher level, so that we work more efficiently and effectively on those tasks that aren't so hard.

- **Put it in writing.** The simple act of putting words on a page (either on paper or your computer screen) allows you to see exactly what it is you have to do, and to prioritise the tasks. As we've seen earlier, the number of things that you can keep track of at once is limited to a relatively small number. Neuroscientists recommend that, instead of trying to keep things in our memory, we should write things down – get it out of our brains and out there into the world. This is called externalising the memory, and it frees up the brain to be uncluttered and to leave space for you to think about the things you really want to think about. So make lists. Write stuff down.

- **Create your own due dates and 'cut yourself some slack'.** You will know in your heart of hearts whether or not you are a good manager of your own time. And since most of us are naturally *not*, why not start to include more realistic due dates with each of your listed tasks, based on your work habits. Build in a 'buffer zone' of extra time for certain tasks: for example, if you know that project X is due next Monday, and it will take you three days to complete, set a cushioned due date of five days rather than three. This will ensure that you start early enough and allow you two days extra to take into account any 'unforeseen' circumstances. If you actually can finish the task within the three days – or even within four – congratulate yourself and feel happy that you have completed it well before the deadline. It really is a case of mind over matter and therefore a much happier and healthier way to look at your work than to feel that you are always working up against yet another tight deadline.

- **Spend a few minutes on a task that you really enjoy.** If you have a really difficult piece of work to complete and you feel stuck or like you are drowning in it – or you are working on a task which doesn't hold your interest at all – consider stopping that task for just 15 minutes and doing something else. Spend five of those minutes making yourself a fresh cup of tea or coffee or going for a quick walk, then spend the remaining ten on a more pleasant or quick-and-easy task. This can help to change your mood, making it easier to continue with the difficult task when you return to it. Quite often, taking a break and thinking about something different for a few minutes can give your brain time to review what you were doing and you can return to it reinvigorated – and hopefully you will.

- **Minimise time-wasting activities.** Make shorter phone calls. Once you have dealt with their queries, thank visitors to your office for their time, and then see them out of the door swiftly and smoothly – don't let them linger. If you need to stand over the photocopier for a length of time to copy some highly confidential documents, take your office mobile phone with you and make a few calls whilst you are waiting for the copying to finish, or make some notes on how to tackle your next tasks.

- **Just say 'no'.** There are only so many hours in a day, and if it cannot be done, it cannot be done. Even the Strongest Woman / Strongest Man in the circus can't do everything all of the time. Admit to yourself that you are human (albeit super human!) and that, whilst you can get an enormous amount of work done, there are times when you just have to say 'no'.

- **Plan a personal treat for your spare time.** Make plans for some special personal time this weekend – it might be a massage, a day at the spa, a haircut, a good movie, a special meal or a night out with friends. Knowing you have a treat planned at the weekend can help you through the next few days, particularly if it is a stressful week at work.

- **Multi-tasking or switching?** When we are doing several things at once, neuroscientists would claim that we are not actually multi-tasking, but switching from one task to another and back again, very quickly. It is claimed that the brain is not consecutively tasking but only sequentially tasking, and that we flit from one thought to the next very rapidly, giving us the illusion that what we're doing is doing all these things at once – but that, just because we think we're doing something doesn't mean we are. Personally, I'm not so sure about this. I know, for instance, that I can read a page of a book whilst singing along to a song on the radio, and that on many occasions when I used to do a lot of audio-typing, transcribing dictation, I would transcribe an audio recording with one headphone stuck in one ear whilst holding a telephone conversation with a colleague via the phone stuck against the other ear – without slowing down my transcription.

- **Use patterns to remember passwords:** Passwords can be the bane of your life, if you let them. One for your online banking, one for your voicemail, another for your ATM card, your Amazon account, connecting into the parent portal at your child's school, not counting your Windows log-in or webmail accounts passwords. It's so easy to mix them up one against the other, or to forget them entirely – and then when re-setting them we often find that each system seems to have different requirements – some insist on at least one capital letter, one numerical digit, one "special" character, whilst others are more concerned with *"must be at least 8 characters"*, *"must not contain any one character repeated more than twice in succession"* or, horror of horrors *"must not be the same as any password used by you in this system in the last twelve months"*. Some passwords are assigned to you – others you must create for yourself. But don't leave them written down anywhere they could be found!

So how on earth can you keep track of them? I asked a group of PAs some time ago what they do to keep track of their passwords. Some said they keep a list stored in a file on their computer. This, one of them said, was all very well and good, provided they could remember the password to the file (if they used a password protect it)! Others said that they keep groups of passwords and / or usernames in files that they store on their mobile phones or on a Cloud storage facility. Which is great, until you lose your phone, someone finds it and then finds your file and hacks into your bank account. So you will need to decide for yourself on what method you use to keep track of your passwords.

Then there's the question of how to actually come up with new passwords... Some PAs reported that they went for patterns: for example, the first letter of each word from a sentence or the first line of a poem – followed by an arbitrary number (their shoe size, their age when they got their first car, the number of children they have, etc.) Others went for mixing-up letters from the names of several loved ones. More still use pets' names or breeds, combined with the year they got the pet. Some PAs advocated adding a letter or two at the beginning or the end of their username to remind them of how they assigned the password for a particular account.

Whatever method you choose for creating a password, realistically you should not use any form of recognisable word – and you ought to not use that password on another account elsewhere, as if a hacker gets hold of your one and only password they have more chance of making things very difficult for you than if you have lots of different passwords relating to your different accounts on different machines, devices, websites, etc.

• **Take breaks at work:** Many of us feel as though we are overloaded and overwhelmed by all the things that are happening and we can't stop work for even five minutes or we'll fall behind…The idea that if we don't take breaks, we are apparently being more productive. The neuroscience literature is very clear on this, and says that we NEED to take breaks, as there is a mode of our brain that is responsible for most of our creativity. the 'default mode network' or 'daydreaming mode'. This is the part of the brain which hits the 'reset' button when you are stressed or have run into a brick wall in your work.

Bearing this in mind, give yourself an opportunity to enter that daydreaming mode every couple of hours or so at work – just for a few minutes. Read something – perhaps an article in a PA magazine or website, listen to music, look out of the window, get up from your desk and walk around, go and get a coffee or a cup of tea, take some paperwork down to the photocopier. Studies show that people who take regular breaks – and in some cases, naps of 10 or 15 minutes , although I'd recommend this only during your lunch break, not the rest of the working day!) — are more productive and more creative in their work, which more than makes up for the amount of time as breaks.

Being strong doesn't mean, however, that we cannot allow ourselves to be human. After all, we each have our own vulnerabilities, and feeling inadequate (when faced with a large project or an enormous 'to do' list) is actually quite a common feeling amongst us – so don't ever feel that you are the "only one" who is struggling with something. Do not hold yourself up against a fictitious view that everyone else is more capable and stronger than you are. If this sounds familiar to you in any way, then the rest of this chapter is particularly for you:

Bravery is knowing the antidote to thinking "I'm not good enough"…

Taking to heart the teachings of inspirational author / researcher Dr Brené Brown.

I had a strange dream the other night. In it, I was thin with a lovely figure and great hair – and my clothes looked really good on me. I had long slim legs, good ankles (no sign of the no-definition calf-ankle "cankles" I've had for years), and a flattish stomach. Oh, and great boobs. In short, I looked fabulous – and in the dream I caught myself staring in a mirror at how amazing I looked. I went to the gym where I worked out for several hours a day, pumping weights and pushing myself beyond limits. I watched what, when and how I ate. Then I heard a yowling noise and woke up, to find one of my cats miaowing next to me for food.

For a few seconds I was disoriented – and I felt that I still looked the same way as I did in the dream. Then the realisation kicked in – no, I'm me, overweight, my hair needs straightening with hot irons in order to make it feel like hair rather than scarecrow straw, plus I have fat legs and a big belly. I don't own a wardrobe of fabulous outfits, I have clothes that fit me and are suitable for their purpose. I'm not rail-thin or glamorous – I'm just me.

Within milliseconds, a huge wave of feeling washed over me. Several years ago I have to confess that this would have been a feeling of guilt, shame or disappointment. However, the feeling that washed over me that night wasn't any of these. It was relief.

Relief that, in my mind, told me "thank God I don't have to keep THAT up every day", that I do not have to strive for something that's so out of my comfort zone and so far away from my settled norm. Whilst I'm working on my weight issues (and believe I always will be – I'm not naturally thin and I like my food far too much to ever be able to reach and maintain thinness without huge effort), I'm happy with the rest of me.

I've come to realise that I don't need perfection and I don't want to give myself a guilty conscience because I haven't achieved it – I spent years striving to be something "better" than I was, to gain approval from others, to find a sense of belonging or a belief of being successful. I've learnt though that I'm never going to achieve perfection and there is no necessity for me to try to do so – and to be fine about saying "that's OK – I'm imperfect, and I'm enough". This is a mantra I've learned over the last four years from Brené Brown's teachings.

Readers: please repeat after me: "I'm imperfect and I'm enough".

I got the chance to briefly meet Dr Brené Brown, one of my heroines, at a talk and book-signing event in London in 2012. For those not in the know, Brené is a research professor at the University of Houston, who has conducted extensive research over more than a decade in the areas of vulnerability and shame – and gave several inspiring talks on her findings at TED shows in the USA.

Brené's treasure trove of more than a decade's research and her findings include evidence that human beings are built for connection, and that this is key to our happiness and sense of well-being. In her TED talks, she asserts that "we are hard-wired for connection".

This has then led to further talks, her authoring of several books, and now she works regularly with Oprah Winfrey, teaming up to run TV and online workshops exploring the principles in her book "The Gift of Imperfection". The main theme of these classes (and that book) is: "I'm imperfect and I'm enough."

I'm aware that I'm repeating that phrase several times in this article, but I'm doing so as I firmly believe it is very important.

In the past five years I've worked with several thousand PAs, EAs, Secretaries and Administrators worldwide – and a staggeringly large percentage have admitted to feelings of inadequacy if they are unable to be the "Super Woman" that their bosses expect them to be – or which they themselves expect them to be.

Many have told me of their worries of not being "good enough" or "clever enough" or "quick enough" to be as good in their jobs as they can possibly be. They strive for perfection, thinking that getting their work perfectly right at all times is an achievable goal, if they could just work hard enough to attain it. They work long hours, take on more tasks than most people in other roles could ever hope to manage, and push themselves to unattainable or unsustainable limits, in the guise of being "indispensable" to their boss or manager. Others have told me that they daren't allow themselves to try something new or different (like a new hobby or a sport) because they feel they won't be good enough. This can extend to preventing them from doing a whole range of things, including applying for a new job, because they have become convinced of their impending failure.

I know this to be true. I've done all of this myself, and more. I've taken shorter holiday breaks than I could have done, as I've felt that the office wouldn't manage without me if I stayed away from work for longer. I've stayed in work during sickness and illness – often to the further detriment of my health, under the notion that "I must work harder" and "I can't go home now, everyone needs me to be here".

I'm so glad that I came across one of Brené's talks on Youtube. I'm even more glad that, after watching it, I then searched for more, and then bought her book, and started to truly believe that, no matter what unattainable perfection I used to strive for, I'm enough as I am. Yes, my hair takes an hour or so to straighten it in order to tame the wildly kinked frizz that I was born with, and it's no longer dark brown but has a large number of grey / white roots which I find hard to disguise with hair dye, but it's a job that's manageable with straighteners or curling spray and I'm embracing being a newfound blonde. I'm imperfect and I'm enough.

Please note: it's not "I'm imperfect BUT I'm enough", as if being enough can negate being imperfect: the whole point is to embrace BOTH parts of the equation – that I'm imperfect AND I'm enough.

I now try to translate this mantra to my work. The documents I work on do not need to be perfect. They need to be good enough to fulfil the requirements of the task in hand. They need to convey the right feeling, the right information, the right purpose. They do not need to be perfect. I do not need to spend my whole day stressing about whether I've got something "just right" or whether I have captured my audience perfectly: I want to spend my time working on projects to the best of my ability but I do not need to push for unrealistic goals and objectives which are out of reach or beyond what's actually required.

The key is to get it right, get it finished, do not hang around perfecting something, and then bravely MOVE ON to the next task. And if you do allow yourself the courage to try something new – like riding a bike or painting a picture – and you find that you are not very good at it, pick yourself up and try something else instead. As long as no-one dies from your actions, there is no harm done!

Readers, please – take out a Post-It note from your drawer, and write on it "I'm imperfect and I'm enough" – and stick it somewhere prominent by your computer. Read it and believe it. You don't have to write it on your hand and show the world, but put it somewhere to remind yourself. All of us in key supporting roles as PAs, EAs, Secretaries or whatever else we are called – we are all IMPERFECT and we are all ENOUGH. And that's a wonderful thing.

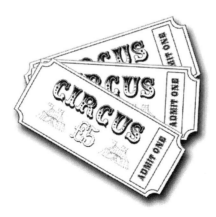

"I'M SEEING AN OFFICE. THERE'S A DESK AND
SOMEONE SITTING BEHIND IT. CAN I HEAR A
PHONE RINGING?"

16. MIND-READING AND SECOND SIGHT

The Mind-Reader: "seeing" what's to come.

"Dear Mind-Reader. What should I do if I could do it all again"?

Hindsight is a fabulous thing. We can all say, after an event, "I wonder if things would have worked out better if only I had done XXXX or YYYY?". But what if you had the power to go back in time and give ourselves some advice to your younger self on the art of being a good PA? What would you tell your younger self to look out for in the future?

I asked this question to a group of experienced Personal Assistants and administrators – these are their answers, including my own...

My tips to my future self:
- Don't sweat the small stuff. Concentrate on the bigger picture and how things fit together.
- Don't take it personally if the boss vents in your direction – they quite often just need to let off steam, it's business, it's not personal.
- Keep track of people you meet in your role – a contacts file / folder / whatever you choose – and make a note of the context in which you meet them, so you have a good reminder source for the future and a great networking handbook! Connect with them on LinkedIn too...
- Make the most of training opportunities – find out all you can, and make sure you use the knowledge you gain.
- A new phrase to me, seen recently in a Twitter conversation – see yourself as a 'Respected Business Partner' to your boss, and do all you can to ensure that they see you in this light too. You are NOT "just" their secretary or their PA or their EA – you are their RBP.

Tips from other PAs:

Marie, Virtual Assistant:
- Don't let people walk all over you – learn to stand up for yourself a bit earlier than I did.

- Keep learning – don't think because you are in admin that's all you can do forever.
- Take on board feedback received in performance reviews/meetings – it is to your benefit.
- Don't take things personally – sometimes people need to vent.
- Don't wear that pink & white checked dress, no matter how good you think it looks at the time!!!

Melissa, Personal Assistant:
- Triple As: articulate, attenuate and amaze your opponents when engaging in conflicting views with reasonableness; you mature as you establish your forte in negotiating different circumstances;
- Triple Bs: bridge, build and brand potential relationships you encounter in every phase of your learning chapters – you never know where it leads you;
- Triple Cs: calm, cool and collected demeanours always generate positive experiences and builds your inner strengths;
- Triple Ds: discuss, determine and decide resolutions adopting 360 degree perspective; you may find flaws in yours to polish and refine for optimal results;
- Triple Es: engage, empathise and encourage your peers and juniors; you may realise that the role model they wished for was just what you had wished in your darkest moments
- Your boss will smile in delight at every moment you present yourself … for you represent him in all aspects!

Kerry, Virtual Assistant:
- Enjoy each step of the journey but don't stew, learn something new to keep the brain alive!
- Don't take everything so personally – people need to vent frustration and the nearest target is normally the one who takes the brunt.
- Be yourself, trust yourself and be confident in decision choices after all you were chosen for a reason.
- Listen to feedback and look for ways to improve and grow.
- Make connections, engage in others and listen. Chances are you will learn something new and build long-standing relationships.

Pam, Executive Assistant / Administration Manager:
- Work hard, be efficient and be very careful with detail = this shows competence and trustworthiness
- Don't take things personally especially when your boss is having a bad day
- Enjoy what you do and give this positive atmosphere
- Always be prepared to help others

> • Remember that your work ethics are 'you' and bosses come and go so always work to your own high standards

Katherine, Secretary:

- Always dress appropriately for the role – black is best (doesn't show the toner on the days when you need to fix the photocopier) and keep a spare pair of tights in your bag at ALL times.
- Always consider any training opportunities and chances to progress – it may not be right for right now, but it will probably be useful at some point. Collect favours and be prepared for a bit of give and take to get what you want.
- Don't be afraid to stand out for all the right reasons – be punctual; be polite; demonstrate your strong work ethic. Be aware that high standards will get you noticed, but may not make you popular. Consider whether those who frequently criticise your performance are similarly gifted and keep a civil tongue in your head when they expose their own limitations.
- Don't wait for permission to develop your own skills. This is one area in which no one else's opinion should matter. If someone is telling you different, they are neither your friend, nor your mentor.
- Do the job that is in front of you, but learn as you go so you can plan ahead – next time the job will be quicker and easier as your skills develop.

Cassie, Executive Assistant:

- Learn to use tools to make your life easier – e.g. meeting invites, calendar + to do list reminders, Google docs/drive – create forms & sheets
- Be sensitive to your boss's needs. It is the small thing that counts e.g. aisle or window seat, black coffee with 2 cubes of sugar, his favourite juice or meal
- Learn to speak out your mind. Do this only when you have process your thoughts & emotions. When reaching out, don't just tell them what you think but also provide solutions
- Be organised. Create systems and implement them for easy retrieval. Information should be at your finger tips
- Learn to ask. Approach people for help if you are not in familiar territories. You will be surprise that people are usually more than willing to give a helping hand

Ana, Executive Assistant:

- Be a leader in your role to other junior administrators, they need mentors as much as anyone else.
- Always dress for success, people notice
- Network, make business connections, send thank you cards and be present in their minds

- Don't be afraid to take a chance...the worst thing that can happen is that you learn a valuable lesson from a mistake
- Treat absolutely everyone with respect, you don't have to like everyone, but everyone deserves to be respected.

Cheryl, Virtual Office Services Specialist:
- Everyone deserves to be respected, including me.
- What I would tell myself is it is not just business, it is personal. You are going to put your heart and soul into it and care about people. You are not a punching bag for anyone and someone having a bad day does not justify his or her bad behaviour. If you allow them to treat you that way by not standing up and saying it is not acceptable, then the only person to blame is yourself.
- Do everything you can to make it a positive working environment, because it is not just you that wants to love their job. If you cannot turn things around so you are working in a professional environment where people respect each other, diversity is really understood, and money does not come before the employees welfare, then leave. Tell the truth when you leave, because it may help the next person.
- I would tell myself to draw strength from my own convictions and take a stand for what is right. Being fired is not the worse that could happen. Ignoring your values is far worse, as it is the same thing as acceptance.
- Tolerance has its place and so does forgiveness, but consistent disregard for what is right – nobody deserves.

Sue, Executive Assistant:
- Know, Like and Be Proud of what you do.
- Know that you are a professional in a business specialism making a difference!
- Never stop learning.
- Never stop engaging with the best new technology can offer..
- There is no "I" in team.

Jackie, Personal Assistant:
- Make sure you liaise with other PAs by way of sharing best practice (both ways I hasten to add!) – I have discovered different approaches to common problems and gained reassurance that other PAs have similar experiences and that, like me, they also still use a 'bring forward' folder!!!
- Sometimes it is just the sharing of our experiences that can help us in our roles, as it can give us a new perspective on things, or a new appreciation of things we've taken for granted about what we do.

Margo, Bookkeeper:

- Always be willing to learn. So much has changed since I started working 40 years ago.
- Always be careful how you deal with people. You never know who know who and how they are connected.
- Your contacts can make or break your future.
- You never know when life throws a curve, which is why education and connections are so important.

Julie, Legal Secretary:
- I wish I had learned earlier to view being an admin as my CAREER, not just a job.
- I would tell my younger self that I'M in charge of my own training, rather than expecting my employer to train me.

Monica, Personal Assistant:
- Remember that the best job of your career may start out rocky and be hard work and misery for the first year to 18 months, so try to give it that long...

Anna, Executive Assistant:
- Network, don't understate the power of it.
- Perception and reputation is everything, keep your personal and work life separate.
- Always learn and keep your skills sharp.
- Pro-activeness, organisation and attention to detail key in this role.
- Learn from your mistakes and own up to them
- Always stay cool under pressure.

Sarah, Personal Assistant:
- Always have a 'can do' attitude when approached by others, you will find that this will repay you at some point in the future.
- Also, never say "but I am just a secretary/PA"!

Juana, Executive Assistant:
- Being a PA is not just a matter of answering the telephone or typing letters.
- The role has changed so much during the past few years. It is really about managing the office and making things happen.
- What I find fulfilling is when I see a successful conclusion to a task or project due to the help and collaboration of all those involved.
- You need commitment to the job, professionalism and trustworthiness.
- One has to be prepared to work hard and be willing to give 100%, keeping in mind that initiative over compliance will make a difference.

ORGANISING AN EVENT NEED NOT BE LIKE A RIDE ON A HELLISH ROLLERCOASTER

17. ORGANISING EVENTS

All the fun of the fun fair: organising events

As a PA you need to be a fantastic organiser. This is a great skill, and something to be highly commended. As you grow and develop within your role, these skills will expand. But when you are first given a large event to manage, it helps to give yourself the best start possible, even if you haven't got all those skills under your belt yet. Here are some of the major things you'll need to take into consideration when organising a large event (like a conference, an AGM, a team building event for a big group, a product launch, an advertising campaign, etc.):

Planning well in advance: do you tend to plan a few months in advance, or just a couple of weeks? How can you work out how long you need to get your event organised? A handy hint for this: use a Gantt chart to develop a timeline for your project.

You can draw a Gantt chart on paper – or you can use a computerised package (there are free packages out there, just search for "free Gantt chart" and check with your ICT team that you are ok to install it on your computer.)

Enter the end date – the date of your conference or AGM – and imagine the final stages just before completion. How long will they take? Mark them in – and then think about the stages just before those. Work backwards from the end date, taking into account all the steps that need to happen, all the people who need to be involved, all the resources that will be needed, items that need to be ordered in (including delivery times), and eventually, you will get to a start point in your timeline.

If the total timeline is less than a month, add in an extra week if you can, to allow for delays and contingencies. In this way, if you don't have any delays and don't need the extra week, you may well get extra 'Brownie points' for coming in quicker than the schedule. If the total timeline is a number of months, add in a couple of weeks at least for delays and contingencies.

It is better to plan for something to take longer than it actually does, so that you have some breathing space, than to be running around like moth near a flame, flitting about helplessly in the final throes and running out of time.

Approach the event like a project: use project management tools to assist you with the planning. SWOT, PESTEL, decision making tools, problem solving devices, the full works. Making sure that your plans are updated constantly throughout the process of organising the event.

Planning Top Ten

Depending on the size of the event – and the size of your company – you may host your events in-house, in which case many of the costs of producing an event can be reduced. If you need to host an event off-site, here is my top ten of tips for negotiating the best possible deals and getting your planning and marketing underway:

Initial planning:

Sign up to the venue holding the date for you, and holding a meeting room – but don't sign a contract yet if you can avoid it.

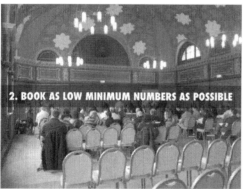

Venues will always be keen to nail you down to numbers. Try to avoid this level of detail until much closer to the event when you have more of a handle on how many people are attending and can adjust your 'held' booking to suit.

A great opportunity to use your negotiating skills.

Example: if the venue offers a Daily Delegate Rate for groups of 10 people or more, ask for a reduced DDR if you are able to bring in 50 people – and a further reduction if your group reaches 100.

Some venues still attempt to include add-ons that many other venues include as standard.

Example: negotiate for free Wi-Fi for your delegates, remove extra fees for audio visual equipment or on-site engineers, ask for drinks to be included in lunches.

Self-explanatory. Keep a really good handle on your budgets and spending at all times when organising your event.

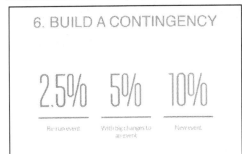

Build in contingency plans: add extra time into the planning period in case it is needed, factor in the possibility of additional costs into your budget.

As soon as you know the date for your event, tell it to your audience. Don't wait for the full finalised plan to be ready before your market – drip feed what you have over a period of time to entice people in…

Don't assume you know what your audience wants or who they are. Research, research, research again.

If you have someone in your team with particular experience which is relevant to this event, USE THEM!

Get in touch with some of your intended audience as soon as you can to find out from them "what do YOU want at the event?" Involve them in the planning, get them enthused about attending.

Two annual events you may be involved in:

A drawback: being the resident 'expert' on organising meetings may earn you one of the unseen 'benefits' of being great at your job: you may be asked to arrange the staff Christmas party or Secret Santa.

To some PAs that I've met, just the words 'Christmas party' and 'Secret Santa' can strike a chord of horror. Not because either task is a horrible one but because it can be so difficult to try to please everybody all of the time.

Please don't get me wrong: both celebrations are lovely sentiments – gathering people together at Christmas and showing each other that you care – but over the years I have found that both can be two of the most frustrating things you come up against. Countless other PAs around the world agree on this, whenever the topics have come up at training events. We all love the IDEA of everyone getting together for a lovely Christmas party and of giving each other gifts to celebrate Christmas, but…. it can be incredibly hard to pull it off without losing more than a little patience and goodwill.

If you are a new PA / EA and haven't yet experience either event from the organisational side of things, you are probably thinking, 'What's so bad about organising the staff Christmas party?' Well, let's see…

- No one can agree on a venue. Someone will always moan that they don't like it, but nobody wants to take the task off your hands.

- No one can agree on what night of the week it should take place – certainly not a weekend night because weekends are sacrosanct, but if it is during the week will anyone be fit for work the next day (because the younger staff are determined to get very drunk)?

- Julie says she will attend the party but doesn't want to sit near anyone from her department (she does like them, you understand, she just thinks she really ought to be socialising with other people).

- Sandra won't have the meal, thank you, but she will sit at a table sipping cocktails and glaring at the waiters all night (because they are confused by her presence and keep trying to offer her food, but don't they know that she is ON A DIET?)

- Several staff will have dietary requirements which are usually manageable, except there will always be at least one person with the most difficult needs (think of a gluten-free, fruit-free and nut-allergic vegan), who will demand on having a version of Christmas pudding produced exclusively for them, then moan that it was inedible, completely ignoring the fact that the venue has gone to the trouble of creating something especially for them.

- The younger staff won't want a sit-down meal, they'll just want to go to the pub for the evening; whilst the older staff want a meal, but don't want to go to the pub.

- The lower paid staff won't want to go to X as it is too expensive; the higher paid staff don't want to go to Y as it is too low-brow for their tastes.

- Three people won't turn up on the night, and someone else will bring an uninvited guest. Somebody else won't have paid their deposit but will turn up regardless and sneak on to a table thinking it is funny to be getting a "free" evening out. You will spend the evening fuming at their bare-faced cheek and rudeness but, of course, you can't bring it up, because it is a party and we're all meant to be having a lovely time.

- Someone will bring their objectionable, opinionated, highly critical and/or very boring partner along and will proceed to annoy everyone else at their table.

- Someone will be unhappy that it ended so early; others will be unhappy that it ended too late for them to nip off to the nightclub.

And don't get me started on the Secret Santa gifts:

- 'I don't like what I received!'

- 'But I spent more on the gift I bought than the one I received!'

- 'Where's my gift? I haven't got one!'

- 'I don't want to be part of this.'

- 'I think we should all donate to charity instead.'

- 'I haven't brought my gift in on time to go into the pot with the others.' (Which results in you then having to go out of your way on the day before the gift-giving to buy three emergency gifts to cover for those that haven't yet arrived, in the effort that everyone will receive something and the "spirit of giving" remains untarnished – whilst you sit there gnashing your teeth and feeling very un-Christmassy.)

Here are some tips to help these activities run smoothly (and save your sanity!):

- Don't try to please absolutely everyone – it just isn't possible.

- If you are booking the party venue, make sure that you know what the budget is per person – and if staff are to pay to attend, check with a few colleagues as to whether the budget you are aiming at is manageable for them.

- Whatever you are planning, ask a small number of colleagues for their opinions to give you some guidelines for your decision-making. If they have been at the organisation for longer than you, ask them what has been done in the past at Christmastime, what went well, what could have been better and if they have any advice for you in organising this year's arrangements.

- You might want to consider doing a survey of the staff to find out what the majority view is – do they want a meal, a dinner and dance, a pub evening, a quiz, a casino night? Obviously, you will inevitably end up with several groups who want different things, but hopefully you can settle on an option that fits for the majority.

- Don't forget the importance of making sure that everyone can get home from the party – a lovely hotel out in the country might be a very nice venue, but not when you have a crowd of people all waiting for the one and only local taxi driver to get them home. If possible, plump for a city centre venue or at least one with good public transport links.

- For Secret Santa, there is quite often a rush at the end to buy last-minute gifts because someone has dropped out or hasn't brought their gift in. Rather than wait for this to happen, obtain some petty cash and purchase a couple of spare gifts in advance. Keep them safely stored in a drawer or cupboard in your office. If they are fairly generic items, you can always keep them in the office to give as gifts in the new year if they aren't needed.

- Don't let other people's disorganisation ruin your day. There are bound to be differences of opinion amongst the staff as to what constitutes a great party, and there is almost certainly going to be someone who complains or does not enjoy the gift they receive via the Secret Santa. Don't stress about this too much – instead, let them know that you sympathise, but reiterate (gently) that it is nigh on impossible to please everyone.

So, what's my main tip to you regarding Christmas events? Once you have organised either the Christmas party or the Secret Santa for the a year or two, if you then start to dread Christmas coming round again because you know for certain that you will want to murder someone three days before the end of the Christmas term (and funnily enough, it will always be one of the same three people who you want to murder each year because they will always be unreliable), delegate the task to someone else next year! If, however, you love doing it, then keep doing it – just remember to have a Merry Christmas!

"NOT MY CIRCUS, NOT MY MONKEYS.
NOT MY CIRCUS, NOT MY MONKEYS.

OH, HANG ON, IT <u>IS</u> MY CIRCUS...."

18. LEADING A TEAM

***The Performing Monkeys: leading a team. So, yes, it IS
your circus, and these ARE your monkeys.***

PAs leading PAs and admins: The results of the 2015 Hays / Executive Secretary "What makes a successful PA?" survey show that 37% of private sector and 46% of public sector PAs and EAs in the UK are responsible for managing other staff – whether this be managing other PAs, other office staff, both, or other staff elsewhere in their organisation. Approximately half (53%) of these directly manage 2 to 4 employees, and a fifth manage 5 people or more.

The PAs and EAs doing the managing are doing it in the early stages of their careers: nearly a quarter (24%) of all PAs and EAs who are still in their first 4 years in role are managing someone – and nearly a fifth (18%) are managing teams of five people or more. The report deduced "this is likely due to the larger number of more experienced PAs supporting managers in larger organisations at more senior levels, and having direct reports may be less of a requirement."

It seems fairly likely that, at some point in your career as a PA / EA you may be given the responsibility of managing a team of administrative staff. However, the average age within the UK for anyone to receive training on how to manage staff is allegedly 42 – so it is extremely likely that, if you are given the responsibility of managing other staff, then you will be doing it without any management training. <Gulp.>

If you have never been responsible for other members of staff before, welcome to your own personal episode of *Fear Factor*! Push your Executive to allow you to attend some formal management training if at all possible, learn from a mentor, find a book, do some research – give yourself as much of a helping hand as you can.

Managing a team: It can be scary to lead a team for the first, second, third or tenth time. Not because you don't have the skills to deal with whatever comes your way – undoubtedly, as a PA / EA in a busy organisation you have all of the skills you need within your toolkit – but because it can take such an enormous amount of tact and diplomacy to lead a team, and such a lot of effort to motivate, encourage and cajole.

It might be helpful to think about various situations and how you might handle them, in order to think about the skills that you already have at your disposal and how you might put them to good use. For example, how would you tackle the following scenarios?

- Trying to persuade a colleague (who thinks they are 'doing well enough, thank you') to attend a training course as you can see that their knowledge or skills are lacking in some way. How would you broach this, in order to keep the colleague on side, and motivate rather than offend them?
- Working with another colleague who is easily distracted by technology, to persuade them not to spend every moment at work trying out new things on their computer, but to find a gentle balance between learning and getting things done, and all the while trying not to crush their sense of purpose at learning something new. After all, we want our colleagues to develop within their roles, but not to the detriment of failing to get any work done.
- Being the 'young office manager' with responsibility for a team of staff who are older than you and who have been with the organisation for far longer than you. It can be scary to take charge in this kind of situation, and to exert a level of firm but calm authority.

I can't teach you the skills needed to manage a team in one chapter – that would be a separate book entirely, or even a series of books. What I will advise is that you listen to and learn from those around you – your senior leadership team, your Executive, and other members of staff: see how they get things done, and how they can persuade others to do things in certain ways. Rest assured that you most likely have many of the skills that you need already.

To successfully manage an office team, you ideally need:

- **Educational / Training conducive to leading:** It is helpful if you have some related education or training under your belt. If you don't have a degree, you can take business, accounting or management classes through a local college or university, or via books and courses on the internet.
- **Organisational and Time-Management Skills:** Keep physical items in their proper places, manage your time effectively and keep track of staff schedules and roles. Your organisational skills will prove critical in completing tasks on time and making sure each day runs smoothly. For example, arrange files, paperwork and equipment to allow easy access by any staff member who needs them. Make sure every office staff member understands his job description and performs to meet company expectations. In addition, create and adjust work schedules to ensure that all tasks get completed on time.
- **Decision-Making Skills:** Make decisions that benefit your company and its workers. Other employees will turn to you for answers to questions and solutions to problems, expecting you to make fair decisions quickly. You might also have to make decisions regarding customer or vendor matters. In addition, you may have the responsibility of interviewing, hiring and

firing office staff members. Refer to company policy manuals when you feel unsure about the best course of action.

- **Maths Skills:** Use your mathematics skills to oversee the processing of orders, creation of invoices, receipt of payments and bookkeeping. You may also have a role in securing or reviewing company contracts and ordering supplies for the office staff and other company departments. Your maths skills will come into play when managing the office's petty cash, as well. Some companies also require office managers to handle employee time sheets and payroll accounts, both of which require math skills.

- **Multi-tasking Ability:** Handle multiple tasks at one time. Often, being an office manager means taking on or overseeing several projects at once while also fielding requests and questions from employees and other managers. For example, you might be called on to settle a dispute, speak to an irate customer, sign for a package and adjust a work schedule all at once. Always pay attention to detail as you work to avoid productivity-impairing errors.

- **Leadership Skills and Fairness:** Model responsibility and productive behaviour. Supervise and motivate your office staff, and treat all employees with the same level of respect. Arrive on time to begin your workday and complete scheduled tasks on time. Demonstrate teamwork by sharing information and resources with your employees. Listen to employee complaints and concerns, making improvements to the work environment when they will increase productivity and ensure that activities run smoothly. In addition, act as a mentor when doing so will benefit the company and other employees.

- **Communication Skills:** Listen well and provide clear input, answers and advice. Miscommunication can lead to confusion and even dissension in the workplace, so good verbal skills play an important role. In addition, good writing skills will ensure that your instructions and written responses are easy to understand and follow. Though much of your communication will take place with company staff, your communication skills will also be important for dealing with customers and vendors.

You can also look at the leadership styles amongst your fellow staff for guidance. Pick out those who you would like to follow, and speak with them – ask them to share some of their knowledge with you.

On the flip-side you can look at those whose leadership styles you don't like – learn from those people to, on how NOT to do it.

"I'M A BIT TIED UP RIGHT NOW,.... PLEASE
LEAVE A MESSAGE AFTER THE BEEP"

19. DON'T GET TIED UP WITH DETAILS

The Contortionist will bend over backwards to get the job done, but knows that they don't have to be perfect

Have you ever been called a "perfectionist" or referred to as "high strung"? These terms are synonymous with people who do their job at a level that is far beyond the norm. And in some instances, borderlines on being almost insane to outsiders.

There is a huge difference between doing what's required and doing what we think is required. Step back for a moment and look at the intensity at which you approach tasks and ask yourself, "is what I'm doing overkill"? One of the most common stressors in our job is the burden we place on ourselves. Do you find yourself redoing another person's work, or doing your own work over and over again until it is perfect? Do you race around the building rushing from task to task? Do you expect others to accommodate your time schedule?

Change the intensity

For one day, try to do everything at ½ the intensity level. Come to work 10 minutes early instead of 1 hour. Don't redo a single project when the first time is "good enough." Keep your enthusiasm while backing off from a hard hitting, high driving approach. You will find you are much calmer, and may even notice a change in how your co-workers and management treat you.

Getting it right

As you become busier and busier, have you noticed that 'quantity' is overshadowing 'quality'? If you are someone who takes pride in your job, then doing it well is one of the goals you strive for every minute of every day. The issue you face is that the more you try to keep this perfect lifestyle going, the greater your chances of falling short, and the more stress you are inflicting upon yourself at the same time. The result is that your self-esteem takes a big hit and then you begin to feel insecure. In reality, being perfect 100% of the time simply isn't possible. So, how can you overcome your propensity to get it right each and every time?

Make a mistake – on purpose!

If you just fell out of your chair after reading that, pick yourself up and keep reading. Fear is the greatest factor that is keeping you on this tightrope of perfection: fear of not knowing when you'll make a mistake, how large the mistake will be, and how you'll recover after it happens.

Why not plan your own mistake and see what happens. Granted, this shouldn't be something that will have monumental ramifications; it should be something small that carries enough weight to get the point across. For example, if you have been requested to bring copies of the agenda to a small, informal meeting, conveniently leave them in your office. Go to your meeting and when someone asks where the agenda is, politely say, "Sorry about that. Let me just run back to my office to grab those." In all likelihood, no one will really say much about it, and if someone does, so what. Allow yourself the opportunity to be 'less than perfect.'

Imagine the worst

When you think about it, we all imagine "what will happen" in certain situations. Yet most of these visions relate to personal tasks: you forget to buy something when you go shopping (and your daughter's dinner may not contain her favourite choice of vegetable as a consequence) or you neglect to pick up the dry cleaning (along with your husband's 'power tie' so he will have to wear a different one), etc. Why not transfer that imagination process to your work?

Honestly, it is because the consequences of a mistake of any type can have a monumental outcome – even losing our job. Again, that just makes the pressure that much more severe for us to be perfect. Understanding the importance of each task you do is key here, and organisation and delegation can be your best friends.

First, become as organised as you can. Know when projects need to be completed, and schedule your time around those projects. If you are consistently over-un with last minute "I need this now" requests, allocate a block of time for those each day.

Next, find a partner at work that you can team with and exchange small tasks back and forth. For example, if Sally does a lot of photocopying, make a pile on your desk of things to be copied and ask her to copy them for you if she is able to. Likewise, if you are a wiz with a particular feature of a program (e.g. mail-merging address labels in Word), tell Sally that you'll get those taken care of for her when her next mailing is ready to go out.

In both instances, you are diminishing the chances for making a mistake. Now you can focus on the big stuff. Select a task on your desk that you feel is extremely important. What makes it so important? That it needs to be done by a particular date, or that it meets a certain specification (number of pages, formatting, layout, etc.), or that it conveys a particular message?

Select the one "deal breaking" aspect for that task. Take a moment, close your eyes and imagine what happens if you completely fail on that one aspect? For example, it's 9:00 am and the task isn't done and your boss is waiting for it. See yourself walking into your boss' office and telling him/her that you don't have it done. Imagine your boss' response: the questions that will be asked ("why isn't it done?") and the chastising you may receive ("I was really depending on you to get this completed"). Explore your feelings when this happens. Are you angry, hurt, insulted, frustrated, etc.? Continue to sit for a few minutes and take in those feelings.

When you open your eyes, you will have lived with imperfection. The result is you are going to feel more control over the situation because you will no longer be envisioning the worst – you've already lived it!

Put mistakes in context.

You are going to falter at some point. We all do and you are in very good company. But take any mistake and put it into perspective. There is a big difference between someone joking and saying, "Yeah! No agendas. This will be a fun meeting" and the boss expressing disappointment by saying, "I was really depending on you to get this completed."

For those situations in which the comments are light-hearted and humorous, come back with something funny such as, "if my head wasn't attached to my body, it would roll away."

On the other hand, when the boss is staring at you from across the desk, compose yourself and say, "I believe that I completed the task the best I could, given the amount of work involved and the turnaround time required. How do you suggest we rectify the situation?" Not only will this show your boss that you can handle situational pressure, but it makes them part of the situation and the solution. (It may also give your boss a wake-up call that perhaps their expectations are unrealistic and, going forward, they may need to rethink how assignments are given and due dates determined!)

So, you've now made a few mistakes and if you do a quick check, all your body parts are most likely still intact. You haven't been ousted, had your pay docked, or alienated anyone. You have officially re-entered that illustrious group called "The Human Race" and we welcome you!

ONE OF THE MOST DANGEROUS ASSISTANT
ROLES IS THAT OF THE KNIFE-THROWER'S
ASSISTANT...

20. WHAT WENT WRONG THERE ?

The Knife Thrower and Assistant must beware any errors. There's no "undo" button on a knife!

Technology and computer equipment – we rely on them to take the strain in our jobs. Most of the time, things run smoothly. We create documents, spreadsheets and presentations, we send emails, we make video conferencing calls, we wave at our colleagues in another office via Skype or Google Hangouts – but what can you do if it doesn't work?

So this chapter is here to help with the question:

What if it DOES all go wrong?

(Also known as **"How can you best help the helpdesk people help you"**)

What should you do when the IT systems go wrong? What can you do to assist your IT team to resolve the matter as quickly as possible or to ensure that it doesn't happen again?

All too often IT helpdesk staff report receiving messages where the caller says "I've had an error message come up, I need someone to come and fix it NOW". Plus, of course, IT problems seem to occur at exactly the wrong time, when you are working to a deadline on a high priority document. (I sometimes think there is an in-built stress / deadline sensor in many computers, which tells the machine to break down at the worst possible moments.)

How the ICT helpdesk can deal with your problem will be based upon a whole range of factors – and the best way you can help them to help you as quickly as possible is to give the right information on the problem: the fullest information you can possibly give. So, let's say something goes wrong with your computer and an error occurs – either an error message box pops up or (horror of horrors) the 'blue screen of death' appears on your computer. What should you do?

A lot of minor computer problems can be fixed by a quick "CTRL-ALT-DELETE" and rebooting the computer. However, this might not be the best solution at all times as you might lose the document you have been working on, and you may think it better to switch to another item on your task list whilst awaiting the arrival of an expert who can help, so you put your hands in the air, move away from the computer, and go and do something else until help arrives.

Hang on a moment though before you do that!

Before you back away from the computer, you need to contact your ICT support team and tell them what's happened. From having been on the receiving side of calls as the most knowledgeable ICT person in a couple of my roles, I ask you at this point to refrain, if possible, from just telephoning the help desk and demanding they "fix things". Before calling them, make a few notes so that you can provide them with the right information to decipher the most likely problem. Don't just phone up screaming "HELP!"

Instead, use the following questions so that you provide adequate details of what you were doing and some information about your computer system, the problem and the environment in which you were working.

So – what details should you be telling your help desk person?

What did that error message *actually say*?

Don't just tell the helpdesk that an error box popped up – tell them what the error box said. When questioned, most users say "I don't remember, I just clicked the 'OK' button and it went away" – at which point the helpdesk engineer is probably banging their head on the desk with frustration. Without being told what the issue is, without being given the full details of how the package reported the error, there is very little that they can do to help. So when an error pops up on your computer screen, pick up a pen and paper – or a camera phone – and make a copy of everything listed in the error box. (Taking a photo of the error message might be the easiest thing to do here as you can send it by MMS or email from your phone direct to the ICT helpdesk so that they can look at the issue. And it is best to take a photo rather than try to do a screen dump on the computer itself, as if the computer has locked up you won't be able to.)

Which program were you using?

It may seem perfectly obvious to you, but if you don't tell the help desk that you were working in Word or Excel or PowerPoint, they will not automatically know that. You need to tell them exactly which package you were using when the problem occurred.

What version of that package is installed on your computer?

The next thing you need to be aware of is that there are many different versions and sub-versions of each package. So whilst you know you have Word on your computer, you may not necessarily have even noted that you are using Word 2013 or Office 365 – and in the background you almost certainly won't know which update or upgrade of the package you are using, or whether it has been automatically patched with an interim fix during an automated update.

Realistically, your ICT team *should* know what software is on your computer and which version – but this isn't always the case.

(A sub-question might arise here: **What are patches?** Software companies release their new products, expecting them to work in particular ways. However, there are often small conflicts which occur within a computer when different packages are installed – perhaps one package is using an area of memory that another package is already accessing, for example. As and when issues come to light, the software companies create workarounds – small bits of computer code – to fix these issues. The workaround is made available by issuing a "patch" which your computer will usually be able to download automatically during Windows updates. These won't be downloaded though if your computer doesn't regularly update itself or you don't allow an update to take place for some reason – some users have been known to report to their help desk "it's really annoying that Windows is updating as it slows the computer down so can the update system be turned off?"!!)

If your computer doesn't have a particular fix installed, the answer to your problems may be a simple as downloading and installing the latest update. Simply setting a "Windows update" running can solve this.

So, when speaking with your ICT helpdesk it would be helpful if you can tell them which version of the package you are using, as this will indicate to them the latest update on your computer. In older releases of Microsoft office, this was simply a case of clicking the Help menu and then selecting About and then reading to the help desk engineer the package number and service pack number which is shown on screen. In newer versions of Microsoft office which use the Ribbon interface, you may have to search further for this information, depending on the actual package... but generally clicking the package's Help button you will find a link to show you which service pack is installed. Painful as they may be, please don't ever be tempted to stop Windows updates from taking place on your computer just to save time: it will save time in the long run if you leave the windows update running to do its job!

Which operating system is running?

As well as informing your help desk on which program and version of the program you were using at the time of the error, it is also important to make sure that they are aware what operating system the computer is running on: Windows Vista, Windows 7, Windows 8, Windows 10, Mac O/S X 10.7, etc. Again, in an ideal environment, your ICT team should know which OS you are using, but it is often helpful for you to be able to point it out to them in your call for assistance.

There are several ways to find out this: the easiest of which is to just pay attention when your computers next starts up: what does the splash screen that displays tell you about your computer? Note this down for future reference...

Each Operating System has different features and capabilities, so you should make sure that you give the correct information to your helpdesk in order to help them help you.

What were you doing when the error occurred?

This is not just a question of "what document or file were you using" but "what were you doing to that document or file?" For example, were you formatting a lengthy document by using the Styles function, or copying and pasting a table from one part of a document to another, or inserting an image into the document header? Were you just typing, or were you saving the document? Letting your helpdesk know this will help them, as they can (if necessary) use this to try to replicate the error to see what has happened and how to fix it.

Let's got back to the error box or blue screen – what happened next?

If you clicked the OK button or closed the error box, did the programme crash and close? Did the whole computer freeze up? Did everything seem to carry on as normal – with the exception that your work was lost? Did any further error messages occur? If you rebooted the computer, what happened then?

Has this problem occurred before – and if so, how often?

Is this something that has happened previously but you are only now reporting it as it has become too frustrating to deal with? Did this issue start happening after another error or was it after some new software was installed on your computer? Does it regularly happen when you do a certain thing, like opening a particular file?

Did you do anything new, just before the error happened?

Did you change some settings or install something? Let your ICT helpdesk know this. It could be that the changes created a conflict with your problem package... Sometimes removing software from a computer can cause problems – for example, Adobe software installs templates which can sometimes cause issues with Microsoft products – knowing that you just deleted a folder of Adobe templates or uninstalled something may be the vital clue your ICT team need.

What, if anything, have you done since the error to try to fix it?

Let your helpdesk engineer know if you rebooted the computer, closed the error box and carried on, restarted the package, deleted a file or folder to try to resolve things, etc. Quite often a genuine computer error (for example, a problem in a piece of software) becomes exacerbated by well-meaning users who unintentionally do further damage by doing something wrong. Attempting to empty the Temporary directory on a computer (to remove temp files) one computer user I know emptied the Templates directory instead, which meant that all their Microsoft products struggled to open correctly as there were no template files for the packages to use. There was no shame in them having done this, it was just a user error and the files were able to be resurrected from the Recycle Bin and put back where they should be – so just admit to what you've done and let the ICT team know what they are dealing with. There is no point trying to cover up or pretend you didn't do something: just tell them!

Has something has been deleted and you can't find a way to recover it?

If you have saved a document over another one by mistake (in other words, you have eradicated the first contents of a document by saving something else using the same file name), all may NOT be lost... *providing* your original document was saved on a network drive *and* that network drive has been regularly backed up, your ICT staff may be able to resurrect a former version of that document – for example, from yesterday's backup files... Be quick to let them know though, as backups are often not kept for more than a few days before being overwritten with new backups, so you probably won't have much chance of resurrecting anything that was deleted or overwritten more than a week or two ago.

Last but no means least: when did the error occur?

Don't leave it til later to tell your ICT team that something happened. If an error screen popped up yesterday when you were busy, tell them there and then. Don't leave it to today to tell them when you are less busy – by which time you have already amended the troublesome document several times over and your machine has been rebooted overnight. Otherwise, it is like going to the doctor today to tell them about a pain you had in your foot last week, but which has now gone away: they have little to work on other than that your foot hurt, and they can't examine the issue in depth while your foot now seems to be fine.

Moral of the tale: be clear in what you tell your helpdesk and give them as much relevant and useful information as you can to help them to help you.

<< SILENCE,
WHILST MIMING BEING IN A BOX >>

21. ACCEPTING CRITICISM

The mime artist: not just accepting criticism but sometimes also holding your tongue

The boss nodded his head around my door: 'Angela, could you just pop in for a moment so I can have a word?'

Earlier in my career, I hated hearing this as I equated 'having a word' with my having done something wrong and there being a telling off on its way. And I was usually right: something I'd done had gone the wrong way or something I'd said had been off-kilter with someone else's view, and I'd then be told what I'd done wrong, who'd taken umbrage against it or how it had affected a project or a piece of work, and what to do about it.

I would sit there in the boss's office, red-faced with shame, feeling inadequate, silently kicking myself and mumbling apologies. I would walk out of the office feeling like I was completely useless, telling myself I would never do whatever it was again.

In more recent years though, whilst I still cringed inwardly at the invitation to go into the boss's office for them to 'have a word' and I still felt some shame at having done something that had been perceived as wrong, I have started to embrace the learning that resulted from the error.

I stopped saying to myself that I wouldn't do it again. Instead, I join in the conversation with my boss to discuss what other options I could have used, working out how I could resolve this sort of thing in the future and listening to the message behind it all: my good intentions and my integrity were not in question. It was not a fault in me as a person, it was something that I had done which could be rectified and worked on.

I'm not saying for one minute that I enjoy having an error pointed out to me – I don't think anyone does – but it is important to be able to develop the type of working relationship with your manager which enables you to talk together about issues. There is no need to just sit there, feeling exposed to criticism and unable to do anything about it.

Criticism is one of those things that's hard to take, but over time it is better to have it than not to have any comments at all about how well you are doing something. I used to dread it; now I look for it. I ask the attendees on my training courses to complete feedback forms, and to be honest when doing so.

(I also add, 'Be honest, but not brutal, please!' to encourage them to give constructive criticism.)

It takes bravery to receive criticism and turn it into a useful learning and development tool.

Many of the PAs I meet on my training courses describe working for managers who seem to criticise them all the time or who never seem to have a word of praise for them. When they ask me what to do, I share Jenny's story with them. She is a PA in the Fast East, who has experienced working for a boss who made her feel like this (she gave me permission to tell her story to others).

Jenny worked for three members of her leadership team – two who praised her now and then for her work, but the third one only ever seemed to criticise her. Unfortunately for Jenny, this was the person who was responsible for carrying out her yearly appraisal. During the first few years of her job, the appraisal meetings were miserable affairs: Jenny felt that she was being told off for the entire time.

As she grew within her role, however, Jenny noticed that the two directors who praised her only ever gave praise to her – there was never any negative feedback at all. As Jenny observed, 'I knew I wasn't perfect and I knew I made mistakes sometimes, but either they never seemed to notice or they didn't care, so their praise started to mean nothing to me.'

This insight helped her to realise that the third director, the one she had thought of as highly critical, was actually the person who was helping her to develop most within her role, pushing her to become better at certain things, leading her towards a higher level of working. She added, 'I started to realise that criticism can be useful, so even when I felt that maybe the criticism I was receiving was a bit too harsh at times, I looked at it differently, trying to work out how best to use it to improve myself and my work.'

Jenny also started to challenge the two directors who only ever praised her work. She said to them, 'Please let me know if I do something wrong or that you are not happy with. I'd welcome your thoughts, and you are not going to "break me" or upset me if you tell me there is something that you'd like me to do better.' She now feels that she has a more respected standing amongst her colleagues and feels much happier about work in general.

Being able to hear critical comments, even to invite them when they are not forthcoming, and to work on them to your advantage is a great skill to acquire. It is also one of the hardest – after all, no one likes to hear bad things about themselves. But it can be an incredibly useful learning tool: if we take apart the criticism that we receive and break it down into manageable parts we can build on it.

Remember, however harsh it may feel, "It's business, it's not personal…"

Being able to separate out the emotional aspect from criticism is a key aspect: using your emotional intelligence. and remembering 'it's business, it's not personal'. The vast majority of criticisms you receive about your work will be about the ways in which you work, how you have done something or what you have said – not about you as a person.

Seven useful steps to receiving criticism are:

- **Listen Respectfully.** When a person is trying to tell you something negative, it is easy to get upset and focus only on the critical aspects of the discussion. You might be tempted to jump into the conversation and deal with the negative points rather than wait to hear what the speaker truly intended. It is best to hear the speaker out, asking only brief questions for clarity, if needed. Give the person a chance to fully explain any concerns that are being described. Maintain a positive attitude with facial expression and body language. Try not to tune out the points you disagree with while staying focused on the entire message. Make a mental note of the point and plan to address it when it is your turn to speak. The person who is speaking to you will appreciate your willingness to get the whole story before responding too quickly.

- **Be Sure You Understand.** In accepting constructive criticism, you will need to understand fully what has been shared with you. You don't have to accept blame or responsibility for something that doesn't make sense or that isn't clear. After hearing what the speaker has to say, take time to ask questions or make comments to confirm your understanding of the situation being explained to you.

- **Acknowledge the Speaker's Point Of View.** As you listen, you may begin to disagree inwardly and eagerly await your chance to respond. But try to put yourself in the speaker's shoes. This can't be easy for them – they may feel uncomfortable about confronting you with something that is potentially negative, or she may be counting on your intelligence and understanding to accept the situation for what it is, a reasonable approach to solving a problem. You would not respect this person if she hid her real feelings or allowed a more serious problem to develop for failure to address it at its root.

- **Don't Become Defensive.** All of us want to be accepted and appreciated for who we are. We are embarrassed and sometimes feel guilty or ashamed when others notice a problem behaviour or a mistake we have made. That's why it is sometimes difficult to come across as one who can accept constructive criticism. But being open to learning and growing is a desirable characteristic in any job position or relationship. Don't feel that you have to "protect your turf" and go into defence mode just for the sake of appearing right—or even perfect. It helps to realise that you have a valuable opportunity to learn from a negative outcome and become a better employee, partner, friend or family member. While you may indeed have useful information that will enlighten the speaker or at least explain your actions, don't share those facts in a self-righteous way. Instead, try to maintain a humble but positive outlook that will make it easy for others to work with you.

- **Avoid Escalating Tensions.** When discussing setbacks or limitations in a person's actions, the potential for escalating tensions is created. When we feel overly criticised or misunderstood, it becomes natural to bring up past issues or current problems that might otherwise have been overlooked. This is not the time to put all cards on the table, though. It is better to focus on the issue at hand and reserve any exchange concerns for a later time, unless they are related to the current issue.

- **Follow Up With Positive Action.** After accepting criticism graciously, accept the responsibility for making changes that will help matters improve. Some people will pretend to accept criticism, but then fail to make the necessary adjustments. Following up with suitable action will show others that you know how to accept criticism and can actually put it to good use, which will enhance your professional image and potentially improve personal relationships. You might even want to keep a written record of any changes that you do make so if the situation is later revisited, you have documentation that demonstrates your willingness to follow helpful feedback.

- **Take the Initiative.** You don't have to wait for others to take the initiative in giving you constructive criticism. You can ask those whose opinion and expertise you trust for advice or suggestions to help you do a better job or avoid making the same mistake. The only dumb question is the unasked one. Let others know if you need help or are struggling before problems become apparent. Most people are more than willing to provide assistance or answer questions to help you do a better job. Ask someone you trust for a performance review at work or for an honest opinion in a friendship or interpersonal relationship. Then be willing to act on that information, if applicable.

It is also crucial to learn how to give constructive criticism to others

Learning to give criticism (or 'constructive feedback' as it is more often referred to) to others is something that you'll develop over time.

For example, you might be managing a project and need to steer a team member in a particular direction when they have gone off course, or you might be responsible for the office team and need to speak to someone about the quality of their work which has gone downhill sharply.

Another example where this is really important is providing feedback to service providers. Say you spend two or three days attending a training course, and at the end of it the trainer presents you with a feedback form to fill in. Aim to give some constructive feedback. If the form has tick boxes for you to show how useful the various sessions were and boxes for comments, as a trainer now myself, I would urge you not to just tick the boxes to say it was 'very good', 'good', 'average' or 'below average', and leave the rest of the form blank.

Whilst the tick boxes are good overall gauges for the effectiveness of a training course or seminar, the person receiving the feedback will also want some information from you about what was good, what was average and what fell below par. Good feedback forms should give you space to include some comments, so use this to really give your views on how it has been for you.

To demonstrate this – imagine that your manager said to you at the end of the week, 'I'm giving you 3 out of 5 for this week,' and then said nothing more, you would want to know why you didn't get a 4 or 5, or what you could change so that you could get a 4 or 5 in the future, wouldn't you?

Also, don't be ambiguous – 'I really enjoyed the course' doesn't communicate what you enjoyed exactly.

What did you enjoy? Being away from the office for two days? Learning in a conducive environment with a great trainer? Meeting other people in similar roles? Having time to snooze on the back row? The great lunches and snack breaks? Put some detail.

You can use this same approach when giving feedback or criticism to colleagues – by all means give marks on a scale to be measured against in the future, but back up your marks with specific useful comments on what was good, what was bad, and what can be improved upon.

♩ ♪ ♫♫

"LYDIA,

OH LYDIA,

THAT ENCYCLOPAEDIA,

LYDIA, THE TATTOOED LADY…"

♩ ♪ ♫♫

22. MAKING GREAT PRESENTATIONS

***The Freak Show's Tattooed Lady knows how to make a
great presentation...***

Flipchart. Posters. PowerPoint. Prezi. Online. Offline. Words. Images. Sound. Video. What makes a "perfect" presentation?

Here are my steps to working out what's best for which occasion, and how best to create an appropriate presentation.

1.   First of all – ask yourself: "What do I mean by 'perfect'?"

- Do I mean "the perfect opportunity to show my skills off", or "the perfect use of software, encompassing everything you could possibly need"?

- Do I want the presentation to be "perfect for the person who will be presenting", or "perfect for the audience" who have to sit through it?

2.   "What's the purpose of the presentation?"

- Know your point – what are you trying to put across, and why?

- Know your audience – don't assume that they want to hear what you want to tell them – research!

- Know your subject – don't attempt to talk like Einstein if you don't know the topic.

- Know your limitations – don't attempt wizardry if you can't do it!

- Know the basics – how to create a decent, readable presentation which supports your key focus.

3.   What to use?

- PowerPoint. Prezi. Posters. Flipchart. Handouts. Decide on which method you will use for the task. Mix it up a bit – don't always use the same thing.

4.   Everyone's heard of "death by PowerPoint".

- If you are going to make a presentation of any sort, make sure that you are kind to your audience – they will want to be interested, not bored to tears, and need to see your point, "get it", and be able to follow it.

5. Unless you are working in a scientific or medical field, or the work *specifically* requires it, don't go for hundreds of detailed lines and slides.

6. Don't embed a huge chunk of a spreadsheet – no-one will be able to read it, even with the biggest projector and largest screen. Instead, give your audience printed copies of the spreadsheet, and have a slide to present the key points from it.

7. Remember two acronyms. KISS – "Keep it simple, silly!", and CISI – "Consistently is SO important". Create simple but professional presentations – your aim should be to try to present well, using your slides / PowerPoint / posters / Prezi presentation as a tool, not relying on it to do all the work for you.

8. Know your presentation backwards and forwards before standing up to speak about it – so nerves can come and go but you won't get lost in the flow. Have a printed copy by you in case the ICT fails!

9. Consistency: use the same format / fonts / colours / styles throughout.

10. Overload – don't overdo it! Use animations, transitions, graphics, bullet points, words, colours, fonts, images, graphs, sparingly. And keep a watch on the number of slides you use!

11. Images / Videos / Sounds: think about why you want to insert images / videos / sounds. What's the purpose / point you are trying to make? Then look at:

    - Will you use embedded or online files? These can be unwieldy or make file size massive.

    - Embedded video clips often have to be re-embedded if you copy the ppt from USB stick to a hard drive on site – so you need to take a copy of the video clip on USB stick too.

    - Online clips might be: blocked (some organisations block Youtube), or not working due to internet problems – or just NOT available on the day as the site has disappeared, in which case you are left with a 'duff' slide, so check thoroughly what facilities will be available if presenting off-site.

    - Quality of items? Does the item really show your organisation in best light? A line drawing, a badly scanned image, an off-kilter photograph, a boring diagram – can all detract from what you are saying.

12. Safeguarding issues: think carefully about using photos that include members of your staff. Make sure that, if anyone leaves – or dies –

then their images are removed from the photo store that you work from. You don't want to send your boss to a meeting somewhere, for example, with photos of a former member of staff included in the presentation – particularly if everyone knows that that person left to work for a competitor!

13. Quality of photos – do you use:

- Your company's own photos – can look posed, static, awkward, can't see what's going on if taken "off the cuff"

- 'Free' images – can look "free", e.g. cheap and nasty, you get what you don't pay for

- Stock photos – can scream "We have an office full of robots" – or "we're too ugly to photograph!"

  Other things to note about images:

- Copyright issues – don't steal from other websites!

- Fashions and ICT can look dated pretty quickly.

- Consider paying a photographer to come into your offices and take properly posed pictures.

- Background colours, background images, text colours – can all interfere with readability.

14. Animations and Transitions: I hate them with a passion. Don't use them. At best they can be cute, at worst they are annoying. They are not business-like. Plus moving items can play havoc with the readability of the presentation and the mood of the audience.

15. Think of your readership. The Board of Directors and the Shareholders most likely do not want to see EVERY single line of EVERY single slide scroll in or fade out, or EVERY slide to appear via checkerboard transition

16. Be realistic. Are you wanting to add transitions and animations to your slides because you think it shows off your skills in using the package, or because you actually think it is going to add value to your presentation?

17. Your organisation should look sharp, clear, focused, on the ball, approachable, easy to understand, transparent. Not cluttered, over-busy, coming-at-you-from-all-sides, panic-led, fluttery/jittery, disorganised, inconsistent or cute.

THE CLOWN'S MAKEUP HIDES THE REAL PERSON BENEATH....

23. WORKING WITH DIFFERENT MANAGEMENT STYLES

Recognising each and every one of the Clowns: working with different management styles

What types of leadership and senior management styles have you experienced in your career so far? Who were your best / worst bosses, and what did they do that made them the best or worst?

Once you've been in a supporting admin role for just a few short years you'll realise and acknowledge that almost every industry and office environment has at least one stereotypical manager or director.

There are many different types of management styles that we are likely to come across – some good, some bad. If you work for one of those in the "Good" or the "not-so-good" category, good for you!

However, there are unfortunately a large number of not-so-good styles that are exhibited by many of our Executives.

Recognising the style of the person you work for (or each of the members of your company's management team) might help you to work better with them in the future, as you can adapt how you to react to their requests / demands to suit their style.

The following are just SOME of the types of management styles I've met / worked for / come across in my career. Thankfully, the vast majority of people switch from one style to another – they aren't just one of these stereotypical typologies:

THE GOOD...

Pacesetter:
expects and models excellence and self-direction.

If their style were summed up in one phrase, it would be "Do as I do, now."

Authority:

mobilizes the team toward a common vision and focuses on end goals, leaving the means up to each individual.

This person's stock phrase is "Come with me." Focuses on objectives and results. Competitive, headstrong and driven.

Affiliate:

works to create emotional bonds that bring a feeling of bonding and belonging to the organization.

Their firm belief is that "People come first."

Coach:

develops people for the future.

They build their teams up by encouraging them: "Try this."

Democratic:

builds consensus through participation.

If this style were summed up in one phrase, it would be "What do you think?"

Participative:

communicates face to face, shares information regularly, involves teams and individuals in making decisions without handing over full authority to the team.

Understands the importance of team spirit, and focusses on asking rather than telling

Creative:

sociable, full of ideas, often flamboyant.

They dislike constraints, rejection, stagnation or detail – so will need a PA / EA who can carry out the necessary nitty-gritty to help bring their ideas to fruition.

THE NOT-SO-GOOD

Perfectionist:

has high standards, is cautious and reserved. Dislikes mistakes, criticism, flippancy or chaos.

Expects everyone working for them to be accurate, explain things clearly, follow up appropriately.

Autocratic:

status conscious, relies on power and position to get things done, rarely delegates, sees flexibility as weakness, unwilling to hold open meetings, focusses on telling rather than asking. Demands immediate compliance.

Their common phrase is "Do what I tell you."

Potty Professor:
wears their glasses on the top of their head and then comes into your office looking for their glasses because they can't remember where they have put them.

No commonsense at all and can barely tie their own shoes, but they are the cleverest person you've ever met. Reasonably harmless.

Micro Manager:
a boss that believes he knows how others should do their job, who can't trust people to just get on with their job and instead micro-manages everything they do.

Will stand behind you and watch your every move, if you let them. Intent on perfection, and unable to delegate.

Baffled Boffin:
similar to the Potty Professor, but has been promoted beyond his or her capabilities, has no clue how to do the job.

Is frankly quite baffled as to how they ever became appointed as a manager, and will be forever grateful for all the help you can offer them. Has good intentions.

Bad Comms:
a boss that is unable to communicate anything effectively, be it the corporate strategy or individual performance feedback – they simply cannot talk at anyone else's level.

Often scientific in background, means well, but simply cannot speak in plain English.

THE BAD....

Mute Manager:
expects you to know what they want, when they want it and how they want it done, without ever actually communicating it to you.

(Also known as the Diffusion and Osmosis Manager – they expect the information to just make its way to you simply by being in their vicinity or next to you, without actually having to speak to you). Looks at you as if you are an idiot when you ask them to clarify anything.

Incapable:
a Baffled Boffin who has moved on to such an extent that they don't care about the job and have lost any respect they ever had from subordinates and co-workers.

Mushroomer:

the kind of manager who keeps everyone in the dark about everything and only feeds you with a pack of lies.

Doesn't share information, for fear of having their ideas stolen or losing credibility. Seems to think that "manager" = "top secret agent".

Over-Friendly:

a boss that inappropriately wants to be your best mate or nearest friend. Thinks the key to managing staff is to be everyone's best buddy. Quite often, have been promoted upwards to manage the team they used to be part of, and try to maintain their friendly relationships with the team members.

Ineffectual as they do not command respect from their staff.

Laissez-Faire:

provides little discipline, avoids making decisions or being held accountable, allows poor performance to go unnoticed, doesn't get personally involved, and doesn't set clear objectives. The manager who doesn't actually manage.

Seagull:

swoops into the office, squawks loudly and dumps a load on your desk before flying out very noisily. A lot of flapping about, often highly strung, "stressed out", "madly busy".

Needs to be almost nailed down in order to get details out of them.

Ego-Centric:

a boss that doesn't care about the people who work for him and is not interested in helping, coaching and developing anyone else but himself.

AND THE UGLY….

Fiery Fuhrer:

rules by fear. Spits fire and brimstone. This type of manager expects you to kow-tow to them, to bow and scrape, and to apologise for your very existence.

Think Meryl Streep in "The Devil Wears Prada", perhaps throw in a little Pre-Menstrual Tension and a bad hair day, and you've got the right idea.

Criticiser:

a boss that is quick to criticise mistakes others make and is unable to provide constructive feedback. Strangely, they will never spot or admit to a mistake that they have made themselves…

Coward:

a boss that takes on no accountability and often hides behind others – whilst happily laying blame at anyone else's door.

Plagiariser:

a boss that takes credit for other people's work or ideas and passes it off as their own (especially to his or her boss).

Will never promote you – they need you as a source of ideas!

Black Cloud:

a really negative boss who just can't seem to say anything positive and instead turns everything into doom-and-gloom.

The type of boss who says "no" to any request for anything, without listening to what is actually being requested.

Kipper Manager:

a two-faced gutless cold fish – useless at managing people or dealing with real-life situations. Would rather pass off your illness as "nothing" or refuse to authorise your time off, rather than admit that you are human and could possibly have a life outside of work.

Will happily play people off against each other.

Ego-Tripper:

a boss that is arrogant, shows off at any opportunity and is in constant need of boosting his or her ego.

If you've ever worked for people who exhibit any of these traits, you'll be all too aware of various leadership styles.

The key thing is to learn from these people – learn how NOT to manage or lead, should you ever become responsible for a team.

For example, what can you learn from your experience of being managed / led by previous bosses, to ensure that you don't become the type of manager you'd hate to work for?

The vast majority of people go to work and get on with it, in whatever style comes to them by default – but we have the opportunity to look at and examine what we do and how we interact with those around us, to make a change for the better.

Going forward, in acknowledging the styles and mannerisms of your Executive, your challenge is to find the best way of adapting your own working methods to suit them.

This is so that you can build the best possible working relationship with them, in order to provide them with the right support for them in their roles.

It is not enough to just be a good PA / EA and have good skills – we strive towards being exceptional, and providing the very best support possible.

THE 'POSTER GIRL / BOY' FOR THE CIRCUS –
THE RIDER ON THE DANCING HORSE

24. BEING AN AMBASSADOR

Riding the Dancing Horse: being a great ambassador for the PA / EA community

We're a hard-working bunch, us PAs and EAs – we're devoted to the role we do – but often to our detriment: we forget about looking after ourselves. Not only do we need to take adequate time for rest and relaxation in our lives, but we also deserve a bit better of a deal than we are getting right now.

You have an important role to fulfil: not just the role at your organisation, but as member of the administrative community – as an ambassador for other PAs and EAs out there.

It is an uncomfortable thing to bring up but I can't write a whole book, encouraging you to be the best you can possibly be in your role, without looking at the truth of where our roles fit in our organisations. PAs and EAs are underpaid, under-recognised and misunderstood by the vast majority of our employers. And we need to change this – all of us within the admin community need to play a part in this. We need to work to improve the lot for ourselves and for each and for future admins who will follow.

The norm seems to be that we work the same long hours as our Executives – or even longer – and we give more of our free time to working in the office than we receive in annual leave entitlement, not counting the hours we spend during evenings and weekends dealing with emails and messages.

We ensure that our Executive's office runs smoothly, we make 'executive decisions' in their absence, we draft or indeed write their correspondence, and we decide who they meet, when and for how long. With ever-increasing tasks and responsibilities we work at manager or director level. We manage our Executives' time and business for them.

Yet we have little recognition for the work we do, our level of expertise, the importance of our role, we receive less training and support than most other roles – and we are paid a tiny fraction of our Executive's earnings.

Your role here is to work with your Executive in an attempt to change this. This is a role for all of us.

Here are a few facts and figures to illustrate this:

The UK National PA Survey of September 2014 gives the most recent information available (at the time of going to press) on the working hours of PAs and EAs.

Does your boss expect you to work outside of normal office hours?		
No	50.1	53.0%
Yes	49.9	47.0%

If yes, how many additional hours a week do you work?		
Under 1 hour	6.1	4.0%
1-2 hours	18.4	11.0%
2-3 hours	17.4	20.0%
3-4 hours	11	
4-5 hours	13.7	23.0%
5-6 hours	8.8	9.0%
6-7 hours	5.9	9.0%
More than 7 hours	18.9%	24.0%

This shows that around half of PAs / EAs are expected to work additional hours than their contracts state – and that a quarter are working for the equivalent of an additional day per week.

It might not need pointing out at this stage, but 7 hours per week is a working day – so over the space of a working year, if we are entitled to 25 days' annual leave, this means we are giving away almost twice this (47 days) in the additional hours that we work. That's more than two working months.

This isn't right.

In exchange for this, we are still seeking recognition for the importance of the role of PA / EA supporting the leaders of our organisations. We still battle with media perceptions of us as shy, timid, quiet, subservient "Miss Jones" types, or the erotic fiction make-believe of the sex-starved secretary. We're paid, on average, the same as the average worker anywhere in the UK – around £26,000 per year. Granted, there are some PAs or EAs out there who are earning substantially more than this figure, but they are in the minority.

News reports in August 2015 revealed that the chief executives of Britain's biggest listed companies were paid approximately 183 times more than the average U.K. worker – and therefore, their PA / EA – during the previous year.

This isn't right either.

The Hays / Executive Secretary "What makes a successful PA?" survey results were released in July 2015. They surveyed more than 2,500 PAs and EAs around the UK and more than 300 Managing Directors and Chief Executives, from organisations of all sizes and across all sectors. The survey revealed that almost two thirds of these senior level employers saw their PA's contribution as "equivalent to either a manager (51%) or even a director (11%) within their organisation. Over 70% trusted their PA's judgement in making decisions on their behalf – 45% most of the time and, impressively, 18% all of the time."

There is clearly, then, a huge disparity what we do and the recognition (both monetary and otherwise) that we receive for it.

This, as with the rest, isn't right.

I'm firmly of the belief that giving away the equivalent of a day per week of our time is not good enough, when held up against the average PA / EA salary, the level of recognition we get for the work that we do. We should all, as PAs and EAs, be campaigning for more recognition for the level of importance of our role and, ultimately, better recompense for our efforts in supporting the leadership of the companies and organisations we work for.

Networking with other PAs and EAs, keeping up to date with latest information from PA associations, pushing forward with our CPD – all of these can assist. So can educating our employers about the work we do – ensuring we have an annual appraisal during which we can update our Executives on just what it IS that we do to help them succeed plays a part here.

Just prior to this book going to press, I wrote the following article on LinkedIn, for PAs and EAs worldwide to share with their Executives:. You might like to share it with yours, along with the rest of this chapter:

Executives: do you know your Assistant's value in running your Circus?

Aug 7, 2015

Can we have a show of hands please?

I have three questions for you...

How many Executives can safely say, in all truthfulness, that you know **what your Personal Assistant or Executive Assistant does** on an average day, or during an average week?

How many of you have spent time during the last few months in meeting with your Assistant to **discuss and agree some strategic aims and objectives for their professional development and progression** within the organisation?

And how many of you have worked with your Assistant to **update / re-write their Job Description / Person Specification** at least once a year?

I imagine the number of hands raised will be pitifully low.

Not because you, as a busy Executive, don't value your Assistant's worth – I'm pretty sure you would admit that you wouldn't be anywhere near as effective as you are in your role without them – but because you more than likely don't feel there is a necessity for any of this, to pay attention to their development.

After all, if they are supporting you now, surely that's enough? There is no need to update their Job Description, or set goals surely?

Wrong.

If your Assistant were to leave this week – say they got another role elsewhere, they became ill, they broke a leg, they moved to another area with their partner, Brad Pitt finally answered their telephone calls (or the injunction against being within 300 feet of Johnny Depp was lifted), whatever the reason – **how would you have any idea who would be the best candidate to replace them, or how to best put together the advertisement for their replacement?**

Yes, you could look at the Job Description from when you hired them. But from the 3,000+ PAs and EAs I've met and worked with worldwide in my training work in the last 5 years, and the countless others I've worked with in my own 24 years working in Administration (18 of those in PA roles), I'm pretty confident that whatever their Job Description was when you employed them, that's NOT what your Assistant is doing now in their role.

Sure, they are carrying out the duties listed – but they will have undoubtedly taken on a whole range of additional responsibilities and duties that they deliver to seamlessly day in, day out. They will have developed skills which closely match YOUR OWN, they have soaked up knowledge FROM YOU about how you do YOUR JOB, they know how to run YOUR OFFICE in your absence without the world falling apart.

And if you think you have a clue what your Assistant does on an average day, then wrong again. There IS no average day for the vast majority of Assistants worldwide, nor an average week.

Recruiting and settling in a new member of staff can cost approximately 9 months' worth of their annual salary. How much can you afford to waste on advertising at the wrong level for a new Assistant because you haven't got an accurate picture of what your leaving Assistant did in order to make your organisation run so smoothly?

The closer you work with your Assistant in aiding and encouraging their development, keeping track of their duties and responsibilities, acknowledging their importance and rewarding them appropriately, and recognising their skills and abilities, the closer you become to creating a Business Partner relationship with them – and the more they will be able to support you to a progressively higher level in your company's objectives.

Research from several sources shows that Assistants are incredibly important within an organisation, taking on roles and responsibilities at far higher levels than those for which they are actually paid or reportedly responsible. For example, the 2012 APA UK survey showed that **Executives credit over 40% of their effectiveness to the support they receive from their Assistant** – and the 2015 Hays / Executive Secretary "What Makes a Successful PA?" UK survey found that **62% of employers credit their Assistant's level of seniority and contribution as equivalent to either Manager or Director level in their organisation.**

Employers – and Executives – take note. Almost every week there is an announcement of a new "app" or piece of software which heralds the demise of the Assistant's role, the latest one being the "Amy" assistant who will send automated emails in order to book a meeting for you.

Can I ask you to think about this seriously for a moment, please? Hand on heart, would you rather put your trust in a piece of software to support you, or work with an exceptional human being – an Assistant who has a keen interest in supporting you, can network with other people on your behalf, can help build your brand for you, and can contribute in your organisation at Manager or Director level?

Treasure your Assistant, and let them know that they are treasured. Let them know that you support and encourage their development, that you appreciate their efforts day in / day out in helping you to lead your organisation to success, and that you value their input and contribution as Ambassadors for you and your brand.

They run the show, your Circus, for you. Without them, the show might not go on.

Oh, and while you are at it, if you consider your Assistant's contribution to be Manager / Director level equivalent, how about acknowledging that by an appropriate pay-rise to match that level of importance and paying them at Manager / Director level?

Because it's all L'Oreal, you know.

We're worth it.

"WORK. LIFE. WORK. LIFE.
KEEP IT STEADY, NOW!"

25. AIMING FOR 'WELL BALANCED'

The Unicyclist: finding that all important "work / life balance"

Maintaining a healthy work / life balance is crucial to being a great PA / EA. If you are permanently exhausted, think that you are at the end of your rope, feel unwell or are 'stressed out', you need to take time for you, to make sure that you have adequate time in your 'real life' outside of work to stay focused and well balanced.

Do you take all of your annual leave entitlement? Many PAs and EAs don't.

Do you turn your phone off when you are away? Again, many don't.

And if you are ill, do you struggle into the office because you are so indispensable that you cannot stay home for a day's rest?

It is paramount that we pay attention to our own lives outside of work, and that we pay attention to any health issues. As detailed in another chapter, many PAs and EAs are giving away two working months of their time each year – for free – by working extra hours in the office. This means it is particularly important to make sure that you actually take time off at some point and give yourself time to breathe and to regroup.

In any busy environment it can be very tempting to leave certain tasks for 'quieter' times (perhaps when the boss is away on holiday), when you will have fewer interruptions. However, not only is this bad planning, because it often means that the task becomes urgent because it has been deferred for so long, but it can also lead to you staying at your desk for longer than you need to and not taking off appropriate time for you during the break.

So, make sure you schedule some time off, and then make sure that you actually take it!

Before you go on your annual leave, it is wise to create a pre-holiday checklist to make sure that you are fully prepared, and aim to finish up whatever tasks you can before you go – to a reasonable extent. Don't work ridiculously long hours in order to clear everything from your desk before you head off for your week on the Costa Blanca or Skegness …

Here are some tips for your taking time-off checklist.

Delegate

If you are a senior-level administrator, distribute tasks among your staff – you will already know who can handle what. If you don't supervise other staff, seek assistance from a colleague you trust, and reassure them that you will return the favour when they go on their annual leave.

Keep a note of which tasks you have delegated to whom, which tasks you have completed and which tasks you haven't, so you will know what needs immediate action on your return. There is bound to be more to add to this list when you get back, but at least this will give you a starting point and will help you plan your first week or so.

Organise minor aspects of your role

If your Executive is going to be in the office while you are away, make sure that you fill up the paper trays on the printers, replace any low toners and order fresh supplies – and let them know where spares are stored and how to change them.

It might be second nature for you to pop the printer open, change the toners and clean the print heads, but when your boss is suddenly inkless it is important that they know how to cope on their own! You might also want to leave a list detailing where you keep office basics like staples, pens and folders.

(I say this from experience, having received 'urgent' text messages from bosses in two of my previous jobs, one asking me how to replace the photocopier toner and the other enquiring where the spare teabags were kept!)

Calendars

Make sure your boss's calendar is up to date, and that papers for any forthcoming meetings are in a prominent place, ready for them to take with them. Ask a colleague to keep an eye on the calendar for you – give them a paper copy of it before you go.

In your absence

Update your boss last thing before you go on leave to let them know what has been set up to take place in your absence. Schedule a return meeting for when you get back, so that you can catch up on what happened when you were away.

Then head for the hills (or the airport!) …

Tidy up

Neaten your desk space. While you are away things will be dumped on it by other people, so it will make it easier on your return if you have cleared your work out of the way first.

Reduce incoming emails

Without doubt, you will find a very full inbox of emails when you return. There are a few things you can do to alleviate this problem:

- Unsubscribe from any email lists you are a member of, or set your account to 'no mail' on those lists.

- Send fewer emails in the last few days before your holiday – and hence get fewer responses.

- Empty your inbox before you go – file incomplete items in appropriate folders ready to be dealt with on your return.

- Set up an 'out of office' reply on your account that thanks the sender for their message and indicates that you are away and the date of your return. Include alternative contacts should they require immediate assistance.

- (Put a similar message on your voicemail on both your desk phone and your work mobile phone, if you have one.)

On your return, allocate yourself a reasonable amount of relatively quiet time to go through the messages that have piled up. Basically, take ownership of your email inbox –don't let it own you!

While you are at it, try to SWITCH OFF your home computer / iPhone / Blackberry while you are away

I used to find this really difficult as I'm a sucker for technology and gadgets and the internet and Facebook and keeping in touch with my friends and reading my email and taking photos and so on…

I would take my smartphone on holiday and connect to free Wi-Fi whenever I found it to upload photos to my Facebook account.

I'd then end up checking my personal emails to see if there were any messages that needed my attention, and then I would find myself thinking, 'Oh, and while I'm doing that, I might as well check my work email account too …'

It is an all too common story: many of us spend part of our holiday time doing more work.

Does this sound like you too? I would love to advise you, 'Put your hands in the air, and walk away from the tablet, iPad, iPhone or Blackberry. You are on holiday!'

It is apparent, though, that this isn't always practical or possible. You worry that the boss might need something urgently, so you just do a quick check – and before you know it, you have spent an hour or so of your holiday time on work-related emails.

So, should you or shouldn't you check your emails while you are on leave?

These questions remain hot topics judging by recent press coverage.

Some PAs are convinced that their bosses need them constantly and that today's 24/7 way of life means that you should be available at all times.

Others firmly believe that no one can really switch off and get the benefits of being on holiday if they are constantly online, so they wouldn't dream of checking their work email when they are away.

How available do you allow yourself to be?

The 2014 UK National PA Survey asked PAs about their holiday habits:

Do you stay in touch with the office when you are on holiday?	
Yes, I check in daily	14.9%
Yes, I check in occasionally	29.5%
I am available if an emergency arises	33.6%
No	22.0%

This means that nearly 45% of PAs either phone in, pop in or check their office email accounts when on holiday, whilst a further third are available for emergencies. Only a fifth of respondents said they kept their holidays completely separate from their work. So what's the best thing for you to do?

It is not just about deciding whether you log in to your work emails when you are away. In fact, both you and your Executive need to be absolutely clear about what is reasonably expected of you.

It could be argued, for example, that you have been given a staff mobile phone expressly so that you can be reached at all times, in which case you need to leave the phone at work so another colleague can cover your role completely when you are away. Be brave. Set some boundaries.

If you or your boss are really convinced that something might occur that is so urgent that you need to be contacted when you are away, and you truly believe that you cannot say, 'No, I will definitely not be available when I'm away,' then go for the middle ground.

Set up a system with your boss before you go, whereby you give your personal email address to your head teacher and tell them that it can be used in cases of emergency or extreme urgency only.

So, for anyone who emails your work email address you will be unavailable, but your head can reach you if absolutely necessary.

However, if you have followed the various tips outlined in this chapter, then there shouldn't be any emergencies because you will have fully briefed your boss and a trusted colleague to take on tasks in your absence.

Have a great holiday!

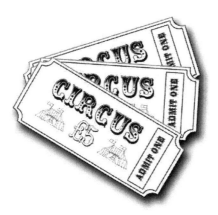

TODAY: THIS TOWN.

TOMORROW: THE NEXT TOWN...

26. <u>WHERE ARE YOU GOING?</u>

The circus truck represents your aims for your next year and how you are going to get there

Have you got your goals and plans together for the next 12 months in your role? More to the point, how can you make sure that all your good intentions and possibilities at the beginning of the year actually continue throughout the rest of the year?

Put some thought into the process – and write it down!

It is surprising how many people either have a vague idea of what they want to achieve or say "all in my head" – and then, when you ask them for details, they don't have any.

Pick a time to start your planning

I tend to do my planning for the year to match the UK financial year – from the beginning of April to the end of March. You might prefer to plan in December, for the new year starting in January – or for any other time of your choosing. Educationalists, for example, plan from September to August. Some companies plan from August through to July.

My start of year, therefore, is the beginning of April – so during the end of March I spend a few hours planning my goals for the coming year and putting them down on paper. I find it best to start this by just brainstorming and throwing any idea out there for ten or twenty minutes, then I start to group them together, rule out the "absolutely impossibles", and then transfer them to a spreadsheet.

I then start filling the spreadsheet out and set about bringing my ideas and thoughts to life by adding some specific actions and objectives which will enable me to reach my goals. This is not just for my role as a PA Trainer, Author and Editor, but a few personal items too – for that thing we often forget about: our "real life".

(I should add at this point, that whatever plans I make during March are not fixed in stone for the next 12 months – I go back to my plans throughout the year and amend them accordingly to take into account new projects and ideas.)

Make it a SMARTER plan

It is all very well having a resolution or goal for the year but unless you know how it is going to happen and the actions you need to take to achieve it, you may not even get started. Write down your actions on a daily, weekly or monthly plan

Use the 'working SMARTER not harder' approach in creating your plan (see earlier in this book for the SMARTER acronym in detail.)

Start slowly

A useful quote to remember is: *"A journey of 1000 miles begins with the first step"* (Lao Tzu, father of Taoism).

If you set off with great but totally unrealistic goals, you are likely to fall at the first hurdle, when you realise that you've bitten off more than you can manage or it is something you are never likely to stick to. Like that well intentioned diet, finishing work on time, spending more time with the family...

Get motivated about your aims

Really understand what's motivating you to achieve your goals this year. Is it because you 'should', it is expected, it is what everyone else is doing or because it is something you really want. How much do you want it? How different do you want your life to be 12 months from now?

I'm against making any New Year Resolutions – how many of us set a really high aim and stick to it for just a few days then forget all about it when it becomes too unrealistic to sustain? What I do is to take a look at my life as it is now, and pick out any things in it that I want to change – then put some appropriate steps in place to start doing something about it – and then start working on it, one step at a time.

Go public

If you tell someone what your goals for the year are, you are far more likely to achieve them.

Accountability can be a powerful driver. Not only have you told someone else what you plan to do but they can check up on you, keep you on track and give you a motivational boost when you need it.

They may even join you if you have a shared goal. You are less likely to let yourself off the hook or forget about them, when someone else also knows.

Get started

Sometimes the hardest thing is just getting started. We tell ourselves all sorts of reasons and make excuses for why we can't do something or why it won't work. Those old patterns of behaviours don't mean you can't change. Once you get started you might find things aren't quite as negative as you thought.

Focus on the little things

Quite often it can be the simple things in life that can bring us the greatest pleasure and sense of achievement. Look around at some of the smaller things you can change this year, not just the big, challenging, life changing goals.

Success builds confidence

As you tick off your successes, you can move on to more, once you see what you can achieve. Don't give up just because you don't get instant results. Sometimes we're too focused on the 'all or nothing'.

Remember it's a 1000 mile journey.

"ROLL UP! ROLL UP!
COME AND SEE SOMETHING TRULY
EXTRAORDINARY – THE INCREDIBLE
BEARDED LADY!"

27. IT'S ALL A BIT WEIRD AND WONDERFUL...

Like the Freak Show's bearded lady – sometimes it can all be a bit weird and wonderful being a PA...

Do you ever receive strange requests from your boss? What's the oddest thing you've done in your role as their PA / EA?

And what has been your proudest moment?

Here is a collation of some of the best responses from PAs in the UK in the 2012 and 2013 National PA surveys:

The WEIRD

(reproduced with permission from the UK's National PA Survey 2012)

What's the most ridiculous thing you have ever been asked to do?

- Oh, where do I start ...

- Rather not say!!!

- A boss's child's homework.....and also a boss's wife's homework for her teacher training course.

- Alter a pair of angel wings so they fitted in to my bosses suitcase.

- Arrange "escort girls" for a boss I worked for.

- Arrange for a sporran to be made out of road kill my manager had found on his estate.

- Arranging an Austin Powers suit!!

- Asked to leave the office to go to my employer's house to collect his wife's purse that she had forgotten and take it to her at Harvey Nichols so she could pay for her 'got to have because they are in the sale' Jimmy Choo's!!

- Asked to sew/repair an MD's pair of trousers as he had torn them and he handed them to me whilst in his 'Mickey Mouse Boxer shorts'

- Assist a former boss with his divorce

- Babysit his children and address his personal Christmas cards

- Book my boss' 18 year old son and his friend's trip to the US. Frankly if he was old enough to go, he should be old enough to book his own tickets.

- Booking a doctor's appointment for a discrete issue they had and having to explain it to the nurse on the phone very embarrassed..

- Buy a batman costume for my boss

- Buy a car with no brief

- Buy a Valentine's Day card for my boss' husband

- Clean bird poo off someone's coat.

- Cover for him to the wife!

- "Do you have any oil for the squeaky door?" I mean, do I look like a mechanic?

- Drive the boss's car to a small village in the middle of nowhere to pick up a batch of hand-made blouses for her.

- Feed a bosses iguana whilst he was away on vacation.

- Feed the boss's hens and put them away at night. Not so much ridiculous as unusual (but very important nonetheless – particularly to the chickens!)

- Find a brace of pheasants!

- Find a particular colour toilet seat for an obsolete range of sanitary ware.

- Get a stray Italian dog a passport

- 'Get me the Minister!' when my previous boss was told he was not allowed to take his hand baggage on a flight after the Department of Transport had restricted all hand baggage on flights

- Go to Fortnum & Mason's in a taxi to pick up moustache wax for a senior partner...

- Help my boss to hide from someone.

- I interviewed for a PA role where they were looking for a PA to drive to the home of the boss to let his dog out!

- I was once asked to make an envelope larger.

- Look after the boss's 6 year old son & 8 year old daughter over the phone! I refused.

- Make sure that I stir his tea in a certain direction.

- Measure up my boss to wear a kilt!

- My boss once said "I'm cold. What should I do?" I told him to put on a jumper!

- Organise a world record attempt for the largest group of people dressed as superman. We did it!

- Personal shopping for wife while running a million pound conference

- Preparing an envelope for an anonymous letter (prepared by a Director) addressed to a member of staff with personal hygiene problems.

- Put staples in a stapler

- Research mortgage options for my boss's daughter.

- Retrieve a briefcase from a closed cafe on a Friday afternoon at 5:30 pm.

- Sit on a squeaky chair, moving from side to side whist my boss was on his hands and knees below me, spraying WD40 to silence the squeaks.

- Sit with a former colleague's dead body in an open casket and read the bible for three

hours (I was a PA in a Camphill Community and their belief was that the spirit took three days to leave the body so each member of the community sat with the body for the first three days, apparently it was a compliment for me to be asked – so I said yes) – It's not really ridiculous but it was quite weird.

- Stay after hours (when 6 months pregnant) to arrange my (old) boss' wife (personal) travel arrangements

- Stop an army band walking across a football pitch

- Syringe boss's ears

- Take my boss's Dad to the seaside for a day out!

- The PA code of conduct wouldn't allow me to tell you that!

- To buy boss's swimming trunks

- To run to the shop and get him a beard dye

- Walk ex-bosses dogs and pick up their mess.

- Write a best man speech

Then we come to:

The WONDERFUL

(reproduced with permission from the UK's National PA Survey 2013)

What has been your career highlight so far?

- Achieving my NVQ 3 in Business Administration with support from the company I worked for at the time.

- Achieving the next level after working so hard and finally being recognised that I am doing the work

- Being able to be dropped into a situation that was new to me and managing to get a positive and effective outcome

- Being head hunted for a very senior position

- Being nominated by my boss to represent our organisation by attending the Royal Garden Party at Buckingham Palace

- Being nominated for a national award.

- Being part of a successful company during a time of great change and seeing the changes

- Being selected as a Rising Star within the business. This is the first time a PA has been selected to take part in this intense development programme and a real defining moment that the perception of the role within the business has changed.

- Current job is a highlight as I work in Publishing and it is the most friendly and accommodating industry I have ever worked in.

- Developing close working relationships that enable boss to flourish.

- Embracing change, lots of it!

- Getting a job as an EA in New Zealand with no experience, just on personality has enabled me to come home to the UK and secure a PA job in the public transport industry.

- Getting the job I'm in now... it may have been a step back, but there seems to be scope for progression

- I had over 12 different bosses in my career to date so I'd say that surviving that is an achievement in itself.

- I would say networking and ongoing development opportunities

- Making my boss 1/3 more productive in his role because of me doing my role!

- Making some great friends along the way.

- Meeting Gary Barlow!!!

- My boss telling me that our peers (his and mine) see us as two halves of a whole, that we are nearly interchangeable.

- One of my bosses said I was the most professional secretary he had had.

- One of the people I support telling me that I was the first person who made him realise what a PA could do.

- Organising a complete office move

- Organising a very large, very complicated Women in Business event.

- Organising the opening of the National Football Centre with the Duke and Duchess of Cambridge

- Rapid promotion and being head hunted in my twenties

- Taking our guests to The London 2012 Games

- There have been so many, it's difficult to think of one specific highlight

- Travelling to Singapore to train a new Executive Assistant

- When my old boss returned to the US the Technology Chief of staff asked me to go and work for him, that's the best recognition of skill.

- Working abroad as a PA to a Finance Director in Bermuda for five years.

- Working at The Body Shop and seeing Anita Roddick in action

- Working for my boss who has just left – he encouraged me all the way to create my own company to train PAs and to push for excellence in all I do.

- Working in a very secure environment for an amazing boss, who supported me in every way possible. There was a good rapport between us and I was allowed to really expand my role to encompass all areas.

- Working with the same boss for over 11 years now and seen him progress into the CEO position.

(Both items reproduced with kind permission from Diversified Communications UK)

THE LION-TAMER STARES INTO THE JAWS OF DEATH, SEEMINGLY WITH NO FEAR...

28. ANNUAL APPRAISALS

The Lion Tamer will put their head into the lion's mouth: adopt this bravery to ensure your annual appraisal is worthwhile

Planning for the year ahead:

In 2015 Hays and 'Executive Secretary' magazine surveyed over 2,000 PAs and 300 managers and found that:

- 0 to 4 years in role: 65% do not have a written plan in place with their manager

- 5 to 8 years in role: 72% do not have a written plan

- 9 years+: 73% do not have a written plan.

As a written plan for the next year would usually be produced in a performance review or annual appraisal, this implies that most PAs don't have an appraisal – or at least, if they do have one, no goals are set in place for the future – but why is this?

Many bosses have little or no idea what their PA / EA actually does – so they have little or nothing against which benchmark them. They also have no idea of what goals to set for the future. In addition, there is lack of recognition of the importance of CPD for their PA / EA which is often accompanied by the fear that "if we train you, you will leave"? There is also a sense of "you are here when I need you, there is no need to write a plan around that".

Lack of recognition of the importance of the PA / EA in their organisation can also play a part ("you're JUST a PA" syndrome) and also many PAs don't challenge their bosses when told they aren't included in the appraisal process.

Annual Reviews are absolutely vital for ensuring development and growth in our roles.

But what if you don't get an annual review? You need to brave up, go to your boss and demand one. Why?

Most organisations carry out some form of performance appraisal / monitoring / annual review of their staff. Sadly, however, the Administrative staff often get left by the wayside during this process.

You may be responsible for the paperwork for your company's reviews – but you might not have an appraisal yourself.

In my training work, I always ask the attendees if they have regular appraisals. With education PAs, I receive a "yes" from only around 20% of attendees, whilst with corporate / industry PAs, it tends to be around 40% of attendees.

Adding this to the number of PAs who don't have a written plan in place for the next year, all of this leaves an awfully large number of PAs and EAs out there who are not being regularly appraised.

Why is it so important to have an appraisal and what's it for?

An appraisal or performance review is your opportunity to discuss with your boss where your role is, how you are doing in, where you want it to go in the future, what their plans and goals are, and to set goals and objectives for your coming year.

- It is for you and your manager to check whether you are succeeding in your role: meeting any targets that have been set, passing any deadlines which have been given, and, most importantly – are you worthy of a pay rise or promotion or change of responsibilities?

- It is an opportunity to set and confirm goals / targets for next year and to clarify any issues surrounding your duties and responsibilities.

- Quite often, bosses will tell us that appraisals are not directly linked to pay, but how many high-performers do you see getting rises as opposed to the low-performers?

- You need to know from your Executive is there is anything you do at the moment that you could perhaps do differently and better. You need to know what they anticipate being the major elements of work that they will need your help within the coming months – and you need to assess whether you have the skills and abilities to carry this out.

- You need to go through your major tasks that you have undertaken in the last year – and weigh up whether your job description needs updating to take these into account. (For the vast majority of PAs and EAs, once you've been in role for about six to twelve months, you are no longer working to the job description that was originally assigned to your role – you'll be working on a whole range of other tasks and responsibilities in addition or instead. This means your job description should be updated to match – otherwise, if you suddenly leave, how will the company know who to appoint in your place, if they don't know what you do in your role?)

What should it NOT be?

- It should NOT be an opportunity for whinges, gripes and moans – either about your job or about other staff. By ALL means bring difficulties and problems to your boss's attention, but have some possible solutions at hand, ready to suggest.

- It is not something that just constitutes your boss saying "I think you're wonderful, I couldn't manage without you". Although it is nice to know that, those are empty words that do not help you one jot.

- An appraisal should either be thorough – or it should not happen at all. There is no point paying lip-service to the process: it needs to be done properly in order to be truly worth anything to the employee, the boss AND the organisation. Don't do it in your office or theirs, don't allow for interruptions, don't answer phone calls throughout, don't cancel the meeting – or if it HAS to be changed, re-book another date and time for it immediately and make sure you stick to it.

Making it happen

So… if you don't currently have an appraisal, you need to push for one. Speak with your boss, ask for an appraisal / performance review. Book it into your diaries, book a meeting room for it, set adequate time aside for it to take place undisturbed – and then set about preparing yourself for it.

How should you prepare for your appraisal?

How your company approaches their reviews may/may not include your input in the preparation process. If you work for an Executive who asks you to provide information for your own review, one of the hardest questions to answer may be: **What have you achieved in the past year?**

Knowing this question ahead of time – e.g., you've been an employee with the company for more than one year (and hence more than one cycle of the review process) – makes it easier to track your accomplishments throughout the year.

If you are a new employee, ask your Executive or the person responsible for HR whether a typical review includes this type of feedback question. But what is an achievement to start with? According to Webster's online dictionary, an achievement is "something accomplished successfully, especially by means of exertion, skill, practice, or perseverance." However, we sometimes have a hard time distinguishing what's simply part of our job versus an achievement. Think of it in a different way: why can't you doing your job successfully be an achievement?

Here are some examples:

- You are responsible for the weekly meeting minutes which must be distributed the morning following the meeting. But you have consistently completed the minutes prior to when they were due. That's an achievement!
- A co-worker fell ill and you had to pick up a good number of her tasks for several weeks. Not only did you do her job, but you did yours as well – and did both successfully. That's an achievement!
- When working on a project, you discovered that there was a major flaw in your company's internal processes. You took it upon yourself to investigate and fix the flaw. That's an achievement! If fixing the flaw saved your organisation big money, that's a BIG achievement (and you should be tooting your own horn with a vengeance).
- After attending a training class/classes, you implemented what you learned so that you do your job at a higher level. That's an achievement!
- Since last year's review, you have worked at improving every area that needed attention. That's an achievement!
- No matter what you do, if you do it with passion and determination, you will do it at a level which surpasses the norm. Whenever you do, consider it an achievement.

So, where is your list for this year's review?

Where did you fall down?

Once you've listed your achievements, follow a similar process to look at things you have had difficulty with during the year. Where did your skills perhaps let you down, or you didn't have enough expertise at your fingertips? Were there any tasks or projects which went wrong because of bad planning, poor scheduling, not delegating tasks to others, poor leadership (either you leading a team or your Executive in leading you)? What areas could be improved upon?

If there are gaps in your skills you need to put a plan in place to improve them – through training, reading, networking, attending a webinar, researching, shadowing someone else – whatever means necessary.

Plan for the future:

- Have you got your goals and plans ready for the next year?
- How can you make sure that all those good intentions and possibilities at the beginning of the year actually continue?

- Put some thought into the process – and write it down!
- Refer to the chapter on planning elsewhere in this book…

For inclusion in your planning:

Whatever your company and whatever level your Executive works at, almost invariably all of them are seeking the same thing from you as their Personal Assistant:

R eliability

E mpathy

S olutions

P artnership

E mpowerment

C larity of Ideas

T ime Management.

These should be integrated with your goals for the year to come.

Appraising others

If you lead a team, you may be responsible for delivering their appraisals, in which case this checklist might help you with planning:

1   Use full phrases for performance reviews.

2   Avoid surprises.

3   Prepare.

4   Do not "pass the buck".

5   Keep it professional.

6   Balance positive and negative.

7   Show respect.

8   Be committed to accuracy.

9   Review your best and your worst.

10   Don't do all the talking.

11   Document accurately.

12   Be a coach to your staff member – show them the benefit of your experience and expertise to assist them with building theirs.

"KEEP LEARNING, KEEP YOUR CPD BALL UP IN THE AIR!"

29. KEEPING UP WITH YOUR CPD & TRAINING

The Seal Trainer: keeping up with your Continuous Professional Development and training

If you have read this far, and all you have done is read, that isn't enough, I'm afraid.

I can offer a training course in a subject, but the attendees won't learn until they start putting it into practice. Until then, they have been trained, but they haven't actively learned…

This means it is not enough to merely read this book. You need to act on it, and do something with it in order to convert the words on these pages into actual learning.

We would be foolish to think that any of us knows everything there is to know about doing our jobs brilliantly. There has to be something more that you could learn within your role that would help you to support your Executive even better than you already do – something that might speed up a process, or a new computing tool that will put you on a par with other staff, customers or clients who are already using it, or simply working on a new task that you have been given.

Over the years, I have met a very small number of PAs, secretaries and administrators who seemed to think they were so perfect in their roles that they did not need to learn anything more (saying to themselves "I am already great") or anything new ("my knowledge and skills may be old but they are great").

I have to admit that I find this quite a limiting approach to working (not to mention life itself!), and I've thought their views of their roles and responsibilities were more than a bit old-fashioned. I am absolutely certain that we all need to be constantly learning new things, not just for our own professional development but to keep up with the next generation, who are part of our school, college or university.

For instance, at a training course in Kenya where I was introducing the assembled audience of PAs to the use of Gantt charts, one PA related that she had just helped her 10-year-old son with his homework the night before – and the homework was to create a

Gantt chart. There I was, training a group of PAs in their thirties (and above) to use a piece of technology that their 10-year-old children are currently being taught to use in school: we HAVE to keep up!

In another example, I recently came across a photo on Facebook of my cousin Ben's baby boy Ace, sitting with his grandpa with a look of fascination on his face, whilst his grandpa (my uncle) showed him something on an iPhone. I recognised something in the look on Ace's face and dug through my old photo albums, where I found a photo of myself in the early 1970s, at the same age, with a similar look of fascination on my face. I was not focused on an iPhone or any sort of new technology though – I was playing with a small red balloon attached to a stick. How times change!

The author, on a good hair day

Ace with his granddad, my uncle Richard

My cousin's son is growing up in a world where it is the norm to own a device which not only enables us to communicate with the rest of the world by phone call, text or the internet, but also play games and take photographs and videos. We have to keep learning to keep up with new advances in technology, otherwise we will be completely left behind.

Hopefully within these pages you will have discovered some aspect of learning that could help you to deal with a certain situation in your workplace, but unless you put those skills into action no change will come about.

You may have seen some time-saving tips and thought, "Those will come in handy", but until you put them into practice, no time will be freed up.

It is the same with your career: you won't move on in your role or new job and a promotion won't land in your lap without you actively doing something about it. It isn't going to happen automatically, no-one else is going to do it for you.

This is what Continuous Professional Development (CPD) is all about – continuing to develop yourself from both a personal and a professional standpoint.

By far the most important aspect of any PA's, EA's, administrator's or secretary's role is to take care of the day-to-day tasks that free up their managers to get on with strategically important tasks. Many senior executives attribute as much as 40% of their productivity to their PA (APA survey 2012), so it is surprising that many managers take the view that training and development for their PA / EA is not a high priority in their business.

We need to maintain relevance and effectiveness in our role. This means keeping up with the latest best practice in the profession and finding ways to improve our boss's productivity. Most managers would not hesitate to sign off regular training for an accountant or HR director, yet they often fail to acknowledge the training needs of the person who holds them safely in a protected bubble on a daily basis!

How much of a struggle has it been in the past for you to get your manager to agree to letting you attend a training course or a networking event/conference/exhibition for PAs? Being able to demonstrate to your boss how much you have gained from undertaking CPD can be the key to getting them to agree to authorising more of it, particularly when they see how exceptional you can be.

In some organisations – particularly in the corporate world – staff are given CPD targets each year. In other words, they are told how many hours of CPD they should be undertaking. Even if your organisation doesn't have CPD targets, it is good practice for you to take stock on a regular basis to check what you have done that could be counted as active learning.

So, what have you done that could be counted as CPD? Remember, it is not just about attending courses… It is about having the willingness to learn, develop new skills and refresh existing skills. In the last year, have you done any of the following?

- Any online learning – searching, researching, webinars;

- Read any work-related magazines;

- Bought (and read!) any work-related books;

- Trained / coached / mentored another PA / EA – either at your organisation or elsewhere;

- Networked with fellow PAs.

All of these should count as being CPD-related – *if* you've done something and learnt something from it, you've developed yourself, then it should be able to be counted.

Be sure to record your CPD, making note of each new skill or technique you learn as well as every time you find a way to do something differently. Get your boss to sign and date the record. You can use this at performance appraisals, pay reviews or job interviews to put yourself ahead of the rest. Then, most importantly, make sure you follow it up and **turn your training into learning.**

As I've said, it is not enough to just go on a course or to read a book – you need to actively use what you have learned and put something into action for change to come about and for effective learning to have taken place.

Hermann Ebbinghaus, a 19th century German scientist, proved that "learning cannot occur without repetition" with his study into how quickly people forget and what to do to compensate for this: his "Forgetting Curve" was the result, hypothesising the decline of memory retention in time. This curve shows how information is lost over time when there is no attempt to retain it – humans tend to halve their memory of newly learned knowledge in a matter of days or weeks unless they consciously review the learned material.

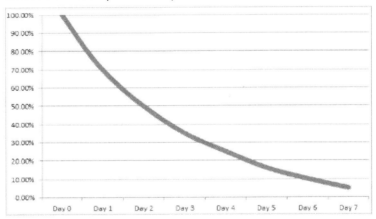

Ebbinghaus's Forgetting Curve – the longer we leave it, the more we forget

A survey of attendees on a 'Personnel Today' webinar in July 2013 asked companies to estimate what percentage of their total training budget was invested in transitioning employees from being simply trained to genuinely learning the content. 95% of the survey's respondents said that they invested less than 10% of their total budget in "ongoing learning after training". Perhaps even more shockingly, 85% of those admitted to investing less than 5% – many of whom privately admitted to investing **nothing at all**.

Unless sufficient time and effort (budget) are invested in this activity, employees receive 'training" but they do not subsequently 'learn' the content of the training course. (Source: "Stupid is as stupid does...!" from http://elephantsdontforget.com/the-facts)

A further review of the survey results indicated that the primary reason for the lack of investment was not a shortage of knowledge on behalf of those staff who had attended courses or undertaken some form of learning activity, but rather failure by their line management to allow them sufficient time or budget for what was regarded as 'unnecessary' and 'optional' activity, in order to put their learning into practice.

Keeping a record

Please use the next few pages in this chapter to make notes on a monthly basis of your learning, decisions and commitments for action: You might like to include dates of training events, conferences and networking meetings, details of books or magazines you'd like to read, training sessions you'd like to offer to colleagues and so on Sign and date the notes, and diarise to check and follow-up on your progress within a month. And remember: keep learning!

MONTH 1 _____

- Things learned:

- Decisions made:

- Commitments for action:

Signed: _____

Date: _____

To be actioned by: _____

MONTH 2 _____

- Things learned:

- Decisions made:

- Commitments for action:

Signed: _____

Date: _____

To be actioned by: _____

MONTH 3 _____

- Things learned:

- Decisions made:

- Commitments for action:

Signed: _____

Date: _____

To be actioned by: _____

MONTH 4 _____

- Things learned:

- Decisions made:

- Commitments for action:

Signed: _____

Date: _____

To be actioned by: _____

MONTH 5 _____

- Things learned:

- Decisions made:

- Commitments for action:

Signed: _____

Date: _____

To be actioned by: _____

MONTH 6 _____

- Things learned:

- Decisions made:

- Commitments for action:

Signed: _____

Date: _____

To be actioned by: _____

MONTH 7 _____

- Things learned:

- Decisions made:

- Commitments for action:

Signed: _____

Date: _____

To be actioned by: _____

MONTH 8 _____

- Things learned:

- Decisions made:

- Commitments for action:

Signed: _____

Date: _____

To be actioned by: _____

MONTH 9 _____

- Things learned:

- Decisions made:

- Commitments for action:

Signed: _____

Date: _____

To be actioned by: _____

MONTH 10 _____

- Things learned:

- Decisions made:

- Commitments for action:

Signed: _____

Date: _____

To be actioned by: _____

MONTH 11 _____

- Things learned:

- Decisions made:

- Commitments for action:

Signed: _____

Date: _____

To be actioned by: _____

MONTH 12 _____

- Things learned:

- Decisions made:

- Commitments for action:

Signed: _____

Date: _____

To be actioned by: _____

HOWEVER MANY PARTS OF US THERE ARE, WE'RE ALL PART OF THE SAME PERSON

30. INTEGRATING THE MANY ASPECTS OF THE PA / EA

The Barnum and Bailey Freak Show's conjoined twins represent bringing all these parts together: embracing and integrating the many parts of the PA / EA

Throughout this book we have been looking at some of the many and varied aspects of ourselves that we utilise in fulfilling many of the various roles and responsibilities of the PA and EA – and I've referred to them individually in their own chapters.

In order to use these aspects to best effect though, we need to integrate them – to combine, amalgamate, merge, unite, fuse, blend, incorporate – and bring them together into one whole.

For the most part, nobody starts off as a 'brand new' PA or EA being able to do this: it is something that builds in us over time, often without us even realising it. We bend, we flex, we adapt to changes and priorities in our workload, and at some point the switching from one task to another starts to come more easily than it did previously, because we've learnt to merge some of our skills and use them all at once.

It's like when we learn to drive a car: we start off being very conscious of every group of actions that we carry out – things like "mirror, signal, manoeuvre", or taking your foot off the accelerator then onto the clutch to change gear then off the clutch and back onto the accelerator. The notion of steering and accelerating whilst watching other traffic – and looking out for pedestrians, potholes in the road and other hazards – seems a lot harder at the beginning than when we become a more experienced driver.

Just think about the average journey you make by car now – for the most part you do not actively think about changing gear or correcting your steering ever so slightly to avoid something in the road, or looking out for pedestrians – you've learnt to integrate those parts of driving into your overall process of controlling the car.

This is what I mean by integrating the various aspects of our PA or EA roles – merging them into our overall process of supporting our Executives.

Whatever the reasons for our going into the role of PA or EA, we generally become successful in the role because of our ability to switch from one task to another quickly and efficiently. This means that the various aspects of ourselves that are so good at the individual elements of our role need to work together so that we can keep a grasp of the enormity of our responsibilities within the workplace.

After all – our Executives are being paid several times more than we are – and in the August 2015 some are being paid 183 times more than we are – and yet we are expected to be able to support them at managerial / director level in their work.

We organise their time, their papers, their meetings, their calls, their correspondence, who they see and when. We put together their itineraries and make sure that they get to the right place at the right time. We tend to their every business need – and in some cases their personal life needs too.

This very often means that we are working on more projects than our Executives, and keeping a hold on more information on more topics than they are – they are in the luxurious position of being able to concentrate on one project at a time whilst we handle all the peripheral information and resources around them.

There is certainly a case here for the PA / EA to be given far more recognition within the workforce for the level of support that we give – and a higher salary to match.

With most managers and executives crediting their PA / EA for at least 40% of their productivity (APA survey, 2012), and 62% of employers in 2015 admitting that they see our level of working as managerial or director level, there is no excuse for this not to happen.

*****

A look at the psychological aspects of being a PA or EA

I recently completed a Post Graduate Certificate in Integrative Psychotherapy.

This was a training programme during which I learnt a great deal about human nature, how we interact with people, how we form relationships with people in our adulthood in similar patterns as in our childhood, and how our early formative experiences influence us as we grow up.

During my studies, I became interested in my own processes and looked at my career to date, and the careers of other PAs and EAs whom I've met during my work delivering training around the world. And I noticed three commonalities, which I believe are aspects that many PAs and EAs have within us (I'm including myself in this) which other people perhaps don't, or which they don't see as important when it comes to choosing their career. I'd like to explore these further at some date in some form of study:

1. DID and switching

Psychologically speaking, it could almost be said that we PAs and EAs have multiple personalities, as we are so well versed in switching from one role to another. Our brains seem to be hard-wired to unconsciously allow us to cope better than most with switching tasks rapidly, and together with our ability to cope with multiple tasks, multiple priorities, and multiple demands on our time: this is on a par with the speed and ease with which a person with Dissociative Identity Disorder (also known as DID) will unconsciously switch from one personality to another.

Please note:

- I am not for one moment suggesting that PAs and EAs all have DID – but I am interested about how our brains switch similarly to those with DID.

- We differ primarily in that we are in control of how and when we switch from one aspect of ourselves in performing our work, whilst a person with DID generally does not have any similar level of control, being mostly unaware of their alternative personalities (known as alters).

- As far as I am aware, no medical or psychological research has yet been undertaken to see if there is any correlation between PAs and EAs with people with DID.

2. Our need to be needed

A second interesting psychological study would be to look at the PA / EA role and what draws us to it – extending from my experiences of talking with several thousand PAs and EAs.

Whilst we all know that our role makes us fairly indispensable to our bosses, there are a number of PAs and EAs who have seemed to particularly relish this indispensability, almost taking delight in knowing that their bosses flounder in their absence – or who have actually reported having felt disappointed on returning from a holiday to find that their bosses have managed without them.

Note: this is very different from simply saying "My boss is lost without me when I'm away from the office", which is very common – what I'm referring to is seeming to want / need the boss to be lost without them and wanting / needing them to flounder in their assistant's absence.

I see this as an over-riding **need to be needed** by our Executives, needing to be indispensable to them and for them to be helpless without us when we are away on holiday or off on sick leave.

I would be fascinated to know how far this observation extends across the PA / EA community, and:

- What makes us go into this sort of role, where we become the be-all-and-end-all for our boss, we control and manage their time, quite often referring to them as "our boys / girls" in a parental fashion?

- Does this need to be needed tie in with our incredibly high sense of satisfaction in our jobs, in comparison with the rest of the working population? (A national survey in 2012 indicated that 31% of workers within the UK are 'content' in their jobs, whilst a second survey in the same year – this time of PAs and EAs only – found that a staggering 82% of PAs and EAs reported being 'content' in their jobs.)

- Is there a link between a certain number of us feeling an inherent need to be needed, needing to please, needing to look after, whilst also needing to feel in control of the person who needs us, and then finding a job where that need can be fulfilled for us so well, as in the PA / EA role?

3. The PA / EA as counsellor / therapist

My third observation that I'd like to look at further in the future stems from the number of Admins who have related to being something of a counsellor within their role: providing a confidential listening space for colleagues, whilst remaining non-judgemental and non-directive.

Whenever I mention this in my training programmes, I see nods and smiles from around the room, in every country: so many of us have had colleagues come in asking "have you got a minute?" who want to have a quiet chat about something that has been bothering them in the workplace, but which they did not wish to take to their own manager or to the HR department. They come to us as they know that we will know what they are talking about, and that we will do our best to assist in whatever way possible to help them work out a solution, and that we will maintain confidentiality on their issue (within reason: there may be some things that we simply have to share with our Executive, but we will tell the colleague that).

This means that our colleagues are seeing us in a counselling role – and many of us are then taking this further by undertaking formalised training.

Our role in supporting an Executive has a very big power / control imbalance – and I personally know a number of PAs and EAs (myself included) who have then gone on to train as Counsellors, Psychotherapists, NLP and CBT Practitioners – all 'helping professions' where somebody else needs us, again fitting with our need to be needed. Within the training programmes we study our own self-development and how to work within a role where we are much needed by clients, but now have the self-awareness to offset any power /control imbalance and can acknowledge our own need for human connection.

*****

These three observations are part of why I think of us, PAs and EAs, as a unique group, as I mentioned in the Introduction.

I'm fascinated by the possible links between who and what we are, and why we go into these roles, as opposed to any other roles elsewhere.

I'm intending on conducting a study in the near future to look into these observations further, as I'd really like to find out more about the PA / EA psyche and what draws certain people to the role of PA or EA over and above another career.

"I SEE A LONG AND SUCCESSFUL
CAREER IN YOUR FUTURE, FULL OF
SATISFACTION AND FULFILMENT..."

31. WHAT DOES THE FUTURE HOLD?

The Fortune Teller: looking forwards to what the future holds for the PA / EA role – and for you in particular

It's always hard to tell what is going to happen in the future, which is why planning is so important. Guesswork and predictions can go awfully wrong at times…

According to one prediction:

Secretaries and PAs will be a thing of the past, they will be replaced by a voice activated robot cart that looks like a mechanised tea trolley. The cart will trundle around the Chief Executive's office, carrying files, phones, and even cups of coffee.

Sound familiar? This was according to an episode of BBC's famous TV show, Tomorrow's World, in 1969.

Here's another prediction for you:

The 'paperless office' is coming. Electronic terminals will be connected to a central database, which will banish letters and printed reports. This prophecy came close to predicting the arrival of the modern computer, but unfortunately fails to understand our continuing love affair with a sheet of paper, complete with hurriedly scribbled, last-minute notes. This was published in BusinessWeek magazine in 1975, the prediction of the paperless office was that it will arrive by 1990.

And we can go even further back with the predictions…. Atlantic Monthly magazine in 1945 predicted that:

by 1960 company directors would run their empires completely on their own, from a huge desk that contained an enormous microfilm library of all of their company's data and would use a voice-activated electric typewriter to send the odd memo. PAs - and all other administrative staff - would be redundant.

How wrong they all were!

Fast forward to 2015: and the predictions about the demise of the PA / EA role are STILL coming. This time, allegedly, we will be replaced by apps such as Siri, OK Google, and Cortana. Certainly, an application here or there can assist in making SOME aspect of a

PA's / EA's role automated – but I genuinely don't believe that any number of apps can replace us.

The latest addition to the string of applications currently offered is Amy. An article appeared on LinkedIn in August 2015 about one of the latest pieces of software to endanger our roles – with the title "This Startup Could Put An End To Personal Assistants". The app, developed by a startup business is an electronic meeting booking device. The theory behind the app was that the developer of the app didn't have his own PA, didn't need one, but said that he was frustrated over booking his own meetings. He claimed that the average meeting takes eight emails to find a time that works for both parties. (*Author's note: eight, really? Has the developer never heard of sending a calendar invite direct from Outlook, or using a shared calendar on Google to allow your invitee to select a date – or, perish the thought, picking up the phone to arrange everything?*)

The app involves an artificial intelligence assistant named Amy. Using the app, Executive A would send an email to Executive B suggesting a meeting and cc-ing the email to their supposed "Assistant", the electronic Amy. Amy will then send automated emails to Executive B, and between them, a meeting date is agreed. According to the article, the development of this app went some way towards the theory that eventually the PA / EA could apparently be replaced.

I responded to the article:

> As a Personal Assistant of 18 years' standing, and now a trainer of Personal Assistants & Executive Assistants globally for the last 5 years, I'm appalled that this article even dares to HINT at the possibility of machinery / technology / apps making the role of Personal Assistant / Executive Assistant redundant.
>
> The Assistant fulfils so many vital roles in supporting their Executive - and one of the major elements of this is NETWORKING (remember, we're all here on LinkedIn for the purpose of networking?).
>
> What possible use could an automated email package be in creating great business relationships with the offices of your rivals, your peers, other companies and organisations?
>
> The Assistant, the real live person, will be not JUST booking a meeting for you: they will be creating a working relationship with other people as ambassadors for you and your brand. They are the personable second voice - both audibly and in writing - of YOU. They know your business inside out, and they know how to negotiate and conduct business

transactions with people at all levels throughout any organisation.

No average Assistant (and believe me, they AREN'T average, the vast majority of Assistants are EXCEPTIONAL at what they do) would go through the rigmarole of the quoted "8 emails" in order to set up one meeting. After the first or second message, they would pick up the phone and SPEAK to someone to arrange - or they would use an online calendar system for the intended attendee (or their assistant) to select a date and time.

Almost invariably, the Assistant supports their Executive in running the organisation without anyone else apparently having a clue about their level of involvement, their importance or their intelligence and vast knowledge of how the organisation works. Creating a piece of software that allows a perfectly co-ordinated calendar to talk to another person's perfectly co-ordinated calendar sounds lovely. But the software cannot and will not replace the necessity for the Assistants who actually co-ordinates and updates those calendars.

In addition, I'm sure that almost every Executive has more than just a meeting to be set up by their Assistant - and there are aspects which "Amy" would be completely unable to assist with. Imagine the following, a fairly typical request from an Executive to their trusted Assistant....

Executive: *"Amy, please book two meetings for me. Don't forget they are across town from each other so they'll need travel time taking into account or matching in with other meetings I have in those areas, and that I'll need you to hand me a pile of papers for each before I leave this office or that you may need to phone one or other of them when I'm late because of bad traffic or that maybe it might be better if we hold a conference call instead to replace either or both meetings, and actually could you check with Bob whether he needs the rest of his team to attend the second meeting, but hey why don't we hold the first meeting here in this building, and if it's on a Friday don't forget to remind the Second in Command in each department that they need to send you their reports for collation beforehand. Actually, forget all that, let's just tell them all to email in, we'll just issue everyone with the project details next week. I'm heading off out now, see you on Thursday. I'm assuming you got all that, Amy"* and the Executive goes out of the door.

Amy: *"Error msg X44468SFJ. Data not found. Please repeat your request and have a nice day."*

Good luck with that.

I'm pretty certain that the role of the PA / EA is here to stay. Yes, the role changes over time and we will undoubtedly use more and more different pieces of software to help us in our jobs, but it's our personal touch that enables the building of great business relationships with our contacts (and subsequently our boss's contacts). No machine can replicate that.

Next time you read an article or hear a report on TV about the PA / EA role becoming obsolete because of new piece of technology X, Y or Z, take a minute to think about what the piece of technology actually offers. It might be that you could utilise it in some way to help you with some aspect of your role – but, pulling together a list of our many duties and responsibilities in order to write this book, it is clear that there are SO many aspects to our roles which would mean that an Executive would need upwards of 30, 40, maybe even 50 different apps to take care of what we do for them on a day to day basis. To which I can only say "no way, not going to happen!"

Executives need to save time not waste it – they want a "one-stop-shop" to tend to their requirements – and that one-stop-shop is their PA / EA. No Executive is going to be happy to use a huge number of applications – switching from one to the other throughout their day – in order to replace us.

For all my disdain over the predictions that software could replace us, most of the software that is out there can certainly HELP us within our roles and assist us to make time savings, find shortcuts or even 'delegate' some tasks (or elements of a task) to an electronic medium. These should, in theory at least, provide us with some space in which we can then grow our roles to take on more strategic responsibilities in working for and *with* our Executives. It is then up to us to push for the recognition we deserve, which will lead to our role becoming Business Partner rather than Assistant, and more respect for our profession from others.

Let's go back to some more predictions, this time from just a few years ago in the hope of finding at least SOMETHING that has come true.

In 2010, Executary News magazine predicted that within the next five years (i.e., by now, 2015):

we will be able to work anywhere from the kitchen to the local café thanks to the next generation of computer technology – so the daily trip to the office will be an occasional treat rather than a regular grind.

Maybe for other workers this can be very true, but in many organisations the Executives still want their assistant to be working in the office with them.

The magazine also predicted that by now we would have *touch and gesture-activated desks that will do most of our admin, revolutionise meetings and networking, and leave us to develop our strategic and management skills.*

Well, we have touch and gesture-activated devices, but not yet desks – those are still, in the main, only found in research labs and on television shows – but the technology has at least been developed for this, it's just not widely available yet.

Within the next five years – that is, by 2020, Executary News also predicted: *3D teleconferencing that will let us have a face to face meeting with a colleague or boss on the other side of the world.*

I have to admit I'm not sure quite why we would need to meet in 3D, when we already have perfectly good systems like Skype or Google Hangout which allow us 2D virtual meetings.

The magazine's final prediction for the future was that by 2020, *intelligent communications software will be able to tell from your tone of voice and body language whether you are too busy to take that annoying call from Berlin – and politely say "no".*

Frankly, I find this idea terrifying! I cannot imagine for a moment that a computerised system will be any better at gauging our mood than humans are – and we all know how easily we can misread the messages that we put out to each other!

When it comes down to it, I'm all for new software that will save us time – but the main technological prediction I've been looking forward to is the new mode of transport which will save us all time and energy in getting from one place to another…

By which I mean, of course, the prediction in the 'Back to the Future' film trilogy that *by 21 October 2015 we will have invented hover boards.* Now THAT's a technological improvement I'd like to see – especially if it could be linked with a satnav device to programme it with where to take me -: it would make no END of difference when I'm trekking around airports dragging my carry-on luggage behind me and I could get to the other end of the airport in no time!

So, technological advances aside, what do you predict for YOUR future? Where are YOU going? What's your plan? And what do you mean, you don't *have* a plan?

Here are a few questions that might help you with making some SMARTER plans for your future – both in your career and in your personal life:

- As a child, what did you want to be when you grew up?

- Are you there yet? What's holding you back from your dreams?

- Were you asked in your interview "where do you see yourself in this role in five years' time?" – and if so, how did you answer?

- Are you THERE yet?

- Where is your role taking you?

- Your company and your Executive will almost certainly have a plan for the next few years but have you thought about whether you have been included in this and in what role?

- Does your exec expect you to still be their PA in 5 / 10 years? How do YOUR plans fit with your Company's planning?

- Where do you *want* to be in five years' time? Ten years' time? What about any thoughts, hopes, dreams or plans for your retirement?

- If you are looking for change – when are YOU going to make it happen? How are YOU going to bring change about?

- If you dream of XYZ happening in your future, how are you going to get it and what might you need to sacrifice or put extra effort in to achieve it?

Opportunities for development

With all of this 'making plans for the future' you might be assuming that I mean you must leave your current company or leave the role of PA / EA in order to progress. Not so. There might be other opportunities in a lot of different areas within your company or to extend the skills you've gained within your PA role into other areas:

- **Continuing as a PA**:
  Increase your existing responsibilities.
  Manage & train other staff.
  Become PA to a more senior person.
  Move to a bigger organisation.
  Follow the boss to another organisation if s/he moves.

- **Moving into other areas:**
  Human Resources,
  Marketing,
  Public Relations,
  Company Secretariat,
  Training,
  Procurement,
  Project Management,
  Medical / Legal / Finance Assistant roles.

Alternative careers

There is always the chance that you are perhaps not feeling as fulfilled in your PA / EA role as you would like, and you may be thinking of something else entirely for your future – a new role, a new career. If this is the case, don't be afraid to dream!

Many people are unwilling to allow themselves to dream of a career where they feel fulfilled and have a sense of accomplishment. But these jobs do exist – and I hope whatever you choose to aim for in your future can become one of these!

I remember seeing a cartoon once in which a man sat on a park bench saying to himself, *'There must be more to life than sitting around thinking there must be more to life.'* and I thought *'how sad, to have nothing to dream about'*.

So, how might you find your alternative career?

Write a list of things you love and are passionate about.

Look at the list and try to decide for yourself what you really want to do.

At this point, don't try to fit it into a specific career, industry type or area – just reflect on your overall dreams and where they fit with your passions.

Then look at how you might possibly incorporate these into your existing role or where they might be available within other roles.

Let go of your fear of change

Many people hold themselves back from new ventures because they fear change, but sometimes just changing your mind can be all it takes to open up the possibility for new opportunities.

Fear can be a strong motivator to staying still, remaining stuck and not moving on, so ask yourself if not facing your fear is holding you back. If so, let go of the fear and see what happens.

Embarking on something new – like starting a training programme, becoming involved in a new hobby or creating a new CV after many years of working in one role – can feel very unnerving , but just think about how much enjoyment you could get from embracing the change, pushing through the uncomfortable period and moving into a more challenging (or more restful!) and fulfilling future.

THE TRAPEZE ARTISTS KNOW THE
PRECISE MOMENT TO LET GO.

IF ONLY THE REST OF US HAD THIS
SKILL...

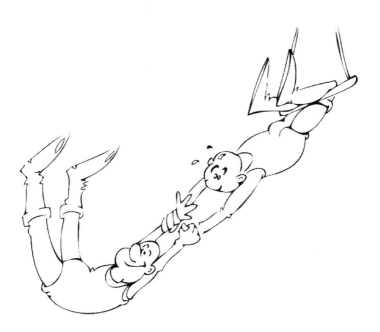

32. DARING TO JUMP

The Trapeze Artiste: daring to jump – from one role to another

As I've said in the last chapter, if at some point you decide that you wish to move on from your role, you might choose to look for promotion within your organisation or otherwise a move to another company entirely.

There are many factors that might influence your career and which could bring about the necessity for change. Changes could happen which you haven't necessary planned for, like an unexpected promotion or sideways move into another role, or a re-structuring / re-organisation within your company. Other changes can be more deliberate like a move to another organisation, a complete shift to a different type of role or a different industry, or taking time out to have a child and then finding on returning to work that you would prefer to be at home with your child…

There are also a whole range of changes that are enforced upon us, which could include your partner being offered a promotion accompanied by a move to another area of the country / the world, your becoming ill or acquiring a disability which means that you can no longer continue in your role, or needing to move to part-time hours in order to care for a relative.

All of these things can happen and cause us to change our plans.

Working out what your new path should be is a difficult process for the majority of us – after all, very few people will admit to actively liking change – and knowing that you have the backing of your boss can be a great boost to help push you in the right direction on your new path.

If you have a great working relationship with your Executive, then both of you will see that it is time for a change for you. They can then support you in the move, assist you in achieving your new goal, steer you towards appropriate assistance and advise you if you are stuck.

If you can both see that your career is moving and progressing, and they can support you in this, then great!

Applying yourself to applying

It can be scary to start filling out application forms, especially if you have been in your current role for some time, and it's therefore been a while since you last applied for a role, or if you are applying for a new type of role for which you don't yet have much experience.

However, if you have a good mentor and a boss behind you who supports your move, they can both lend a hand by reading through your application for you or giving your some pointers on how to apply.

The great working relationship you have with your Executive will now come up trumps: especially if you are working with them in an empowering relationship (where they allow you to have a free rein over what you do and how you handle situations, allowing you to make the necessary decisions).

They should encourage you to take charge over where you are going with your career, and support you wholeheartedly in it. If you are fortunate enough to work with a great boss in this way, you will find that they will quite often back you to the hilt in your attempts to bravely move onwards and upwards in your career.

Whatever you decide to aim for, you will undoubtedly need to put in an application for the new post or position. However, I am not going to tell you how to apply for a job – that would be the subject matter of an entire book: there are so many aspects to presenting yourself in the best light on paper, by email, by telephone, at interview, etc. It is not the aim of this book to show you how to apply for a role – but I will share some tips to assist you.

My main tips when applying for promotions or new roles – or re-applying for your job during periods of restructuring:

- Always think **"how can I show that I am the best person for this role?"**. When I applied for my last role, so did 95 other people – all of us competing for one role. This is becoming more and more common – hundreds of people applying for a role. This means that you need to make your application stand out – for all the right reasons.

  Hopefully you will by now have gained a lot of insight into your own skills and abilities, your strengths and weaknesses, and how you might improve these through Continuous Professional Development. These should all be very useful to include within your application process, in order to demonstrate your suitability for a role over and above other candidates.

- Ensure that you **tailor your application to suit the position**: consider recreating different copies of your CV to send out with your applications for different types of roles. Depending on your skills and the type of roles you are applying for, you might want to create a "Marketing Assistant" CV and a "Chief Executive's Assistant" CV, in addition to an "Office Manager" CV, for instance – with each of these specifically showing off the particular skills that you have which would assist you in those particular types of roles.

- **Vow to tell the truth, the whole truth and nothing but the truth**. Never, EVER lie on an application form – this can be a sackable offence in many organisations. A large number of companies now pay for applications and qualifications to be checked – so don't falsify your exam results or previous employment details.

- A very simple one – **make it look good.** I've dealt with recruitment in virtually every single one of my positions in administration – and, although I hate to say it, I've come across a huge number of hideously bad applications or CVs. Very few could be graded A+ for being visually attractive, written with detail and expertise (read: functional), and for correctly highlighting the most important points of a person's career. If you can work towards this with your applications or CV, fabulous. You'll also get bonus points if your CV is two pages or less!

- **Go in, battle ready**. In days of old when battles were fought and lost via the sword, the average sword fight lasted between 8-15 seconds. This was just long enough for an opponent to find a weak spot and strike. Recruiters and employers will form an opinion of your application within just as short a time. Don't let a weak spot be apparent in your CV or application – make sure that you strike forward with a positive message about your skills and experience, positive messages that you can back up at interview.

- **Don't forget your online presence**. Way back in 2009 Microsoft reported that they checked 70% of applications against the candidate's online presence to see if what they said in their application matched what they said to the rest of the world. More and more companies worldwide are now following suit – so you should be sure to nail down the privacy settings on your Facebook profile to "Friends only" (nobody wants their prospective boss to find 'dodgy' photos of them online...), think before you Tweet (on Direct Messages sent via Twitter are private, and everything that is sent via a standard tweet is searchable via Google) and make sure that your CV closely matches or mirrors what's on your LinkedIn profile. Learn to use social media to your advantage by using it to follow blogs for the companies you wish to work for and increasing your own presence by answering questions in LinkedIn discussion groups and posting sensible discussions and articles.

- **Utilise your skills when creating your application and CV.** If you are a fan of the TV show "Friends" you may recall an early episode when the friends helped Rachel to fold, envelope and stamp a large pile of copies of her CV which she was sending out to prospective employers. On reading it, one of the friends noticed a typo on the CV – where she claimed that she had *"excellent compuper skills"*. Proof-read your applications and consider getting a friend or mentor to check through them with you before you hit "send"! If you are sending documents by email make sure that they are correctly formatted – don't, for example, have a line of spaces where you could have reasonably added a new TAB stop, and don't include lots of line returns to take you to a new page when you should be inserting a manual page break (by using the shortcut CTRL+ENTER). I've seen some horrific documents pass my desk in my time – make sure that yours puts you forward in the best light possible – if you can operate a computer well, SHOW IT!

- **Prepare yourself thoroughly for any interview.** Have a list of questions that you want to ask about the company – check their website to see if there is a CEO's blog where you can gain insight into the latest projects –or check the CEO's LinkedIn profile to see if they have posted any recent articles of interest – and bring these up in your interview to demonstrate that you have an active interest in the company.

  Be prepared for a range of different questions that will be asked of you – discuss these with your mentor, work out how you best like to respond to certain questions. DO NOT learn and recite responses by rote though! A good question to ask is what your interviewer finds exciting about their role – find out more about them, show an interest in what they are doing, see where you could fit in and demonstrate this.

- **Make the most of a phone interview.** Some employers like to hold a phone interview as part of their shortlisting processes, and use this to decide who they would like to then see in a face to face interview. This is becoming particularly common with administrative roles – after all, if they offer you the role, you are going be the first point of contact for your Executive or possibly the company as a whole. A phone interview can determine at least whether you are the type of person they want answering the phone.

If you are given a phone interview, it may be useful for you to stand or walk around throughout the call – and make sure that you smile while you are speaking. It is said that a smile can be 'heard' – so if the interviewer can tell you are pleased, comfortable and enthusiastic without being able to read your body language, you are on the right track. Practice with a friend. Ask them to interrupt you each time you add filler words like "um" or "er" – then practice not doing it. Watch news readers and announcers on TV – the more practiced of them take a breath or extend a word slightly in place of "umming" or "ahhing".

- Remember – **everyone you meet when you attend for an interview is important.** Greet the receptionist warmly – and if there is spare time and they are not run off their feet, approach them and ask what they enjoy about working for the company. In my experience, many organisations ask their Reception staff for their opinions on candidates.

- **Have your phone already turned OFF when you enter the building** – do NOT sit and fiddle with it in reception, as this can imply that you have a poor attention span or that you have something better to do than being there. Pick up some literature in the reception area to look at – or look through the interview papers that you have brought with you.

- **Look and sound confident** – give a firm handshake when you meet your interviewer. No limp dead cold fish handshake here, please – grasp their hand firmly (but not painfully tightly) and give it a firm shake up then down, then release. A weak handshake can feel uncomfortable for both the candidate and the interviewer: again, practice with a friend or mentor.

- This might sound odd, but **do enjoy your interview**, if you can. You are applying to work there, not applying to go in every day and be terrified of everybody – so try not to be terrified by the prospect of having an interview.

Again, I'm not going to go into the interviewing process and beyond here – that also is for another book – instead, let's skip to the good bit, when you have been offered (and have accepted) the role, and you have used your exceptional negotiation skills to agree on an appropriate salary, you then need to prepare for a professional exit from your current role: see the next chapter!

TAKE A BOW FOR THE
CURTAIN CALL

33. PREPARING FOR A GREAT FINISH

Taking your Curtain Call: preparing for a great finish

If you are leaving your role, you need to make sure that the ending of your job is done professionally. Think about what will happen when you are gone. Will any of the staff left behind know:

- your passwords to get into various items of work?

- how to access your documents?

- their way around your filing system?

- how to carry out the major tasks of your role?

No matter if you leave under friendly terms or acrimoniously, a good PA should always leave adequate handover notes behind to allow someone to pick up the pieces after you've gone.

Create Your Purple Folder – The PA's "Bible"

On all of my training courses I talk about the importance of building your Purple Folder – an enormously useful folder of resources which can be used in this situation, as well as many others. To my mind, every PA should have a purple folder. The one and only purple folder in your office – a standout colour, easily spottable – on your shelf. The purple folder is the Bible to your job.

Quite often, one of our biggest worries as PAs and EAs in busy organisations is that we are indispensable – our Executives simply cannot manage without us. Whilst it is lovely to feel appreciated and to know that the work that we do is vitally important to the boss and to the organisation, this can bring difficulties.

For example, if you feel SO needed by your boss that you cannot possibly go off on sick leave, or you cannot take your holiday time, of you are considering delaying having a family for a year or two because there'll be no-one there who is able to do your job as well as you do while you are gone, then you need to do something about it. And fast!

Get moving before illness (or LIFE!) catches up with you – by setting up a purple folder – your job bible – and fill it with detailed instructions of how to do various aspects of your role, including lists of things to be done at particular times of the year, useful contacts, where you file things, passwords to particular websites or computer packages that you know and use on a day to day basis – in short, everything that's needed if you are not in the office for whatever reason.

This means when you are taken ill, you break a leg, go on maternity leave or holiday, or even leave your role to go onto pastures new, the person who next sits down at your desk can pick up the purple folder, look through it, and get on with covering your job or starting their new role in your old job.

Not only is the purple folder the perfect handover folder for changing jobs, but it is also the key to listing your achievements at your yearly performance appraisal as it lists all the major tasks that you do – giving great evidence when the boss says "so what have you done this year that you are particularly proud of?".

Why a *purple* folder?

Two reasons:

(a)   Most offices are filled with single-colour folders and files – all black or all green being top examples. So, having ONE single solitary stand-out folder on your shelf that's a completely different colour makes it easy to tell a boss or colleague or temp from your sickbed how to cope without you. You simply tell them "all the info you need is in my purple folder". When there is only ONE purple folder amongst all of the many folders on the shelves in your office, your boss or colleague has a fighting chance of finding and selecting the right one!

(b)   Purple's my favourite colour.

So... how do you set up your Purple Folder?

1.   The first simple starting point is to order a purple folder from your stationers. Buy a pack or two of dividers too – so that the pages can be separated into sections. As you go on, you will see that this list of sections can get quite long – so I'd advise that the folder you buy is a lever arch one rather than a smaller D ring binder!

2. Start creating sections and add a piece of paper in each listing the things you think ought to go in that section. Some examples are:

    • Opening section describing the role, who you work for, details of the leadership team, members of the rest of the admin team (including who does what);

    • Copy of the company's yearly calendar;

    • Details on how to access your computer files – username, password, file locations, etc.;

    • Daily tasks (which can include subdividers for specific Monday, Tuesday, Wednesday, Thursday and Friday tasks if need be);

    • Weekly tasks;

    • Monthly and annual tasks, perhaps subdivided into quarters 1, 2, 3, 4;

    • Major contacts (including leadership team, admin team and board of directors);

    • Other useful contacts within the company (reprographics, IT support, reception, catering, etc.);

    • Major outside contacts and suppliers (stationery suppliers, drinks machine suppliers, local taxi company, the company you use for booking travel and accommodation, suppliers of your furniture / fixtures / fittings, etc.);

    • PA contacts at other local companies, your sister organisations, other offices within the group, international offices, etc. – and the Executives they work for;

    • List of regular meetings that the boss attends – both internally and outside – and the Chairs of each group with contact details – plus details of any papers that you regularly need to organise / chase / collate for these.

3. Rather than trying to make a completely exhaustive list of sections, stop and think about the last week or the last month – what regular tasks have you done? List them and put this list into the appropriate section – it is the contents page for this section.

Start by writing up one or two tasks per day if you can – you shouldn't be going into massive detail – just a write-up describing the task, what your approach was, how you carried it out and what further steps might be needed later. If you want to handwrite it, that's fine, but you'll probably find it easier to type it as you can include screen dumps (pictures of what you did and how) as useful reminders. Start each task on a new page.

A good PA or admin assistant stepping into your shoes (whether temporarily or for a new role) should be able to work out how to do the things you describe, so don't spend forever going into minute detail.

4.   Aim to write up between 5 and 10 tasks in a week, just setting aside 10 to 15 minutes a day. Some weeks you may find you only get a couple of tasks written up in this time but in other weeks you may get several more done as they are shorter to write up, so don't panic. As you finish writing up each task, print it out and add it to your folder – and add the title to a contents sheet at the front. This way, anyone going through the folder can search by either the contents list or how regularly a task comes along.

5.   Keep steadily working through the daily, weekly and termly tasks that you've done, covering all the regular ones – and making a few notes on those "odd" tasks that seem to crop up here or there – they might not happen again but how you went about solving them could help someone to resolve another odd task when it comes along.

6.   Review where you are up to and congratulate yourself every now and again – you are well on the way to having written your job bible! Look at the sections you've done and see if there is anything that needs moving from one section to another (as in "ah, that comes up more often than I thought, I'll move it to the Weekly section").

7.   Some of the sections will be quicker to fill than others – e.g. your Contacts sections, as you'll probably have all the details you need in Outlook so it should take very little time to copy and paste into a word document to create a list of major contacts. Plus things like staff lists, organisation charts, internal telephone lists, etc. should already be in existence so they can just be printed out and inserted into the folder.

8.   If you think of new sections or new items to add to sections jot them down, one per page, and put the pages into the folder. Don't worry if you haven't time to write them up

yet – the pages will serve as a reminder of items to write up when you do have time.

So... Your folder is in preparation, you are working on it week by week. Now what?

Tell people about it.

One major part of making your purple folder work for you is to tell two groups of people about it – namely, your fellow PAs or admin staff at your school – so that, in the event that you are off they already know to check in your folder as to what regular tasks they could be helping to cover while you are away.

The second group you should inform is your senior leadership team – including your boss – so that they know you are doing all you can to have contingency plans in place in case you are off sick, on holiday or change jobs.

Use it for reminders throughout the year of what you need to get done and when.

If you have put your items into your folder in daily / weekly / termly order, you can see at a glance what tasks you need to get done at the same times year in, year out.

Use it to inform your next appraisal or performance review.

Go through the folder before your annual review or performance appraisal, to give yourself a reminder for listing all your numerous achievements throughout the year. Having a listing of major tasks you have carried you out easily available can prompt your memory – for many of us, our jobs in schools are so frenetic and so busy that it is difficult to think back to what happened in the year and to be able to pick out instances of things you did particularly well.

An additional section you may like to add to your purple folder would be a section for any "thank you" messages or notes of particular praise or accolades.

That's a lot of work to do. What if I am leaving soon and haven't created the whole folder yet?

For starters, your purple folder will be an ongoing item – and should never really be considered to be 'finished'. For now, though, let's concentrate on one section of that folder which will make sure that you leave at least some vital information for your successor: those all-important handover notes that I told you (in the first chapter) to look for when you started your role.

Your handover notes and steps to carry out should include:

- your computer log-in details – including username and password;

- details of where your computerised documents are normally stored (this may be the hard drive of the machine, or a certain area on a network, or a combination of areas, depending on the item);

- if any files are password protected, give the passwords to an appropriate-level member of staff;

- remove any of your own personal files from your computer / network;

- as a courtesy, you could consider leaving your mobile / cell number so that you can be contacted if there is a query about anything.

It is a good idea to prepare this information in advance, even if you are not thinking of moving on at the moment. In this way, if you are head-hunted, suddenly struck ill, have a big win on the Lottery or are affected suddenly by redundancy – or if you DO decide to move on and start applying for jobs elsewhere – you are already partway there to leaving adequate handover notes.

Obviously, if you are leaving the organisation due to redundancy or restructuring, it can be very difficult to consider these things – which is why preparation beforehand (i.e. working on your purple folder throughout your role) is key.

In many roles you are likely to have the opportunity to work your entire notice period – but I've known some organisations who have required certain staff to leave immediately after giving their notice or being made redundant, on the basis that they deem the work that the staff member carried out to be highly confidential or commercially sensitive.

What else should you do before leaving?

Help your boss to put together a decent advert for your replacement along with an appropriate job description and person specification – if you've been keeping these up to date regularly during your time in the role this should now be a relatively easy task.

Depending on the timescales, particularly if you are leaving on a long notice period, you may even have some input into appointing the right person for the role and have a short handover period with them.

Leaving in a professional way gives you the option of returning to work for the same company or boss again in the future (over the years, I've had offers of working again with no fewer than four of my previous employers – including two who now worked at completely different organisations).

Even if you don't take up a job offer from a previous employer, just knowing that they would happily hire you again can be a huge boost to your self-confidence when you come to apply for a new job.

It is also something to mention at interviews elsewhere, so that your prospective new employer will realise what a valuable employee you could be to them, so valuable that your previous employers would have you back in a heartbeat.

What do you need to take with you?

I'd always recommend that you keep a copy of your Favourites list or Bookmarks from Internet Explorer / Firefox, plus your custom dictionary file and autocorrects (both of which will be stored in a hidden Microsoft folder if you are using Word). These can be absolutely vital in your next role, in helping you to get set up quickly on the computer you use there.

"DON'T LOOK DOWN. LOOK TO THE SKIES, AND REACH FOR THE STARS""

34. MOVING ONWARDS AND UPWARDS

The Tightrope Walker: moving onwards and upwards, whatever you do

Finally, we reach the end of this book. Congratulations for getting this far – and I hope you have found lots of items of interest which will help you to develop further within your role!

So many other chapters could have been included in this volume, looking at arranging meetings and travel, creating marketing materials and working with websites and social media, specialising in areas like conveyancing or finance or legal or medicine, being flexible and adaptable (and prepared for anything), providing great customer service, to name just a few. I started out with a list of almost double the number of chapters in this book – but for a PA / EA setting out in their role, I thought 34 would suffice for now.

Please do take note:

This has not been a book designed to change you from being a PA or an EA into something else. It has not been my intention to tell you, *"Yes, yes, you are an exceptional PA / EA now, so it's time to move on to something else now."*

The whole point of me writing this book has been to demonstrate that whilst it is quite possible that you are already absolutely brilliant in your role, there is always something more that you can learn.

Whatever your role is, always be looking to build your skills, to develop the knowledge that you have, so that you can provide the best level of support possible to your Executive. As I've said many times throughout, we can learn an enormous amount from each other in our roles as PAs and EAs so network with others and impart your knowledge and expertise in return for some of theirs.

Working with a mentor, something else I've mentioned a few times, will be invaluable to you in aiding your development and clarifying where you are currently headed in your role.

Whether you stay where you are within your job, move onwards and upwards to a promotion within your existing role or to another role elsewhere in your organisation, or move on to something else entirely, my aim has been to show you that there is always room for improvement, always something different and new to be striving for – and there is certainly something that we can leave behind as a legacy to those who follow us

In each role that I've worked in, I tried hard to ensure that I have left something of me behind: passing on some of my knowledge and learning to other team-members in the organisation, or having set up a process or procedure which has outlived my time there.

My wish is that you will always work towards leaving a legacy of some sort – even if you plan to never leave.

There will always come a time when you are no longer in the role – after all, we all have to retire eventually, or maybe one day Brad Pitt / George Clooney / Johnny Depp / whoever might finally walk into your office and say *"leave all this behind and come with me"*… No? Oh well, we can but dream.

I've loved each and every role that I've held as a Personal Assistant and within Administration in general – and I hope that you feel that too about your role. I've met PAs and EAs who have said that they love knowing they make a difference and that they hold a role of huge significance in ensuring that the organisation runs smoothly.

I hope you can reach this level of satisfaction, and that you gain the recognition that you deserve for what you do. After all, credit where it is due!

From my training work around the world, it is very clear that PAs, EAs, Secretaries and Administrative Assistants worldwide are a hard-working and committed group of very talented people. You are a part of the group – hold your head up, and be proud.

Make sure therefore that you leave something of yourself behind, and make sure that the others who follow you know that they too can be part of the PA / EA Circus.

My parting words to you are to remind you that it is not enough for us to be merely good in our role as a PA / EA.

The world moves on at a dizzying place and in order to "stand out" as the best candidate for a new job or for promotion or for anything else in our lives, we need to be constantly pushing ourselves towards being exceptional.

After all, like the phrase in the fashion world that brown (or grey or navy or whatever is the latest colour) "is the new black", "exceptional" IS the new "standard".

My very best wishes to you for your future.

Now, go out there and…

MAKE YOUR CIRCUS EXCEPTIONAL, AND WRITE THE TICKETS TO YOUR FUTURE!

"THERE ARE A FEW THINGS TO HELP YOU ON YOUR WAY..."

RESOURCES

Some fantastic resources for helping in your work are your colleagues – and the PAs and EAs you come across in other organisations – network with them and use each other as sources of inspiration, advice and guidance. So make you make the most of the people around you – and make sure that you give something in exchange.

To assist you further, I'm including a range of PA / EA related magazines and books, networks and websites, to help you to add to your skills bank.

Do please make sure that you actually *use* these resources though – there is no point in buying a load of books and magazines and having a shelf or filing cabinet drawer full of stuff if you haven't read them or at least dipped into them from time to time!

The items on the next few pages are just a few examples of some of the best of what's available to you.

Magazines are available direct from their publishers and all of the books are available to buy via online via Amazon (among other retailers).

If you attend PA conferences and events, you may find that authors will be there with copies of their books for sale, so buy a signed copy for posterity. It is also a good opportunity for you to network with the authors and exchange business cards (GET SOME PRINTED!)

As you find more great resources, make a note of them in your purple folder and pass the details on to colleagues to help them too.

<u>*Magazines*</u>

NAHPA – National Association of Headteachers' PAs

www.nahpa.org.uk

Editor/owner Angela Garry. Subscription-based magazine, 3 issues per year. For PAs and administrators in schools in the UK and Ireland. Contains no advertising.

Having written for the magazine (under its previous owners) since 2010, and edited it since 2012, I took over ownership of the magazine from April 2015 onwards. Articles are sourced from a range of people worldwide – PAs in education, former PAs, PA trainers, pupils, teaching staff, etc.

Also includes a private group space on LinkedIn, so that subscribers can share information / ask questions of each other and the website has a subscriber-only section with information on training courses, resources, latest trends, and details on guest writers for the magazine. Branding: "NAHPA is the UK's leading publication for PAs and administrators in education".

Coming soon:

UNIPA – a sister magazine, for PAs working in Universities.

Due to be launched in 2016.

Executive Secretary www.executivesecretary.com

Editor/owner Lucy Brazier. Subscription-based magazine, 6 issues per year. A training journal-style magazine for PAs globally. Contains no advertising.

Training articles from the world's top trainers for Administrative Professionals. ExecSecLive is held in March each year – a conference for all PAs from all industries and backgrounds. Check the website for details. Website contains back issues of the magazine which are available to subscribers only – over 500 articles and 100+ transcripts from #adminchat training sessions. Branding: "The essential training resource for senior and aspiring administrative professionals".

PA Life www.palife.co.uk

Free magazine, 6 to 8 issues per year. A glossy magazine for PAs in the UK. Contains advertising from a range of suppliers.

PA Life produce annual comprehensive and dedicated guides which are designed to assist the busy PA with everything from finding the perfect conference venue, to car hire and worldwide travel. Website contains venue search and supplier search facilities, plus details of PA Life's own training days and ExecSec Summit events, where Angela Garry has been one of the featured trainers from 2012 onwards. Branding: "The UK's leading title for personal and executive assistants".

Executive PA   www.executivepa.com

Subscription-based magazine, 6 issues per year. Glossy magazine for PAs in the UK (with sister publications in Asia and Australia). Contains advertising from a range of suppliers.

Holds an annual awards competition, in conjunction with Hays, for PA of the Year.

Website contains back issues of the magazine which can be viewed online for free. Branding: "the longest established and leading magazine brand for professional PAs".

PA Enterprise   www.deskdemon.com

Free magazines available digitally by pdf file only. 11 issues per year.

Subscribe via their website – the UK and US versions of the site and magazines contains some changes. The website includes an archive of all previous issues. Branding: "DeskDemon's magazines for Executive PAs, Office Managers and Secretaries".

Books to help with your continuing professional development

(A to Z by surname):

Baker, Heather (2010). Speed Writing Skills Training Course: Speedwriting for Faster Note Taking and Dictation, An Alternative to Shorthand to Help You Take Notes (Lancashire. Universe of Learning).

Baker, Heather (2012). Successful Minute Taking and Writing: How to Prepare, Write and Organise Agendas and Minutes of Meetings (Lancashire: Universe of Learning).

Barron-Stubley, Susie (2012). Create a Business-Busting Partnership With Your Assistant: The Executive's Guide (lulu.com).

Egan, Marsha (2008). *Inbox Detox* (Boston, MA: Acanthus Publishing). (with blog at http://inboxdetox.com)

France, Sue (2012). The Definitive Executive Assistant and Managerial Handbook: A Professional Guide for Leadership for All Secretaries, PAs, Office Managers and Executive Assistants (London: Kogan Page).

France, Sue (2009, third revision: 2015). The Definitive Personal Assistant and Secretarial Handbook: A Best Practice Guide for all Secretaries, PAs, Office Managers and Executive Assistants (London: Kogan Page).

Garry, Angela (2015) *Brave PAs* (Crown House). (Details at www.bravepas.com and www.angelagarry.com)

Low-Kramen, Bonnie (2004). Be the Ultimate Assistant: A Celebrity Assistant's Secrets to Working With Any High-Powered Employer (New York: NK Publications).

Schwartz, Laura (2010). Eat, Drink and Succeed: Climb Your Way to the Top Using the Networking Power of Social Events [Black Ox Press, The].

Seeley, Monica (2011). *Brilliant Email: How to Win Back Time and Increase Your Productivity* (Harlow: Pearson Education). (with blog at www.mesmo.co.uk/blog)

Sokol Evans, Vickie (2013). 10 Tips in 10 Minutes Using Microsoft Office 2010 (Tips in Minutes using Windows 7 & Office 2010) Plus at least 5 other titles in the same series.

PA-related and training-related websites – all for FREE!!!!

<u>www.alison.com</u>   A training website offering diploma courses online. Create a free registration to use the site and sign up for a course. Free use of the site includes advertisements during your course sessions, or you can choose to pay for a premium subscription which will not include the advertising.

<u>www.bookboon.com</u>   An absolutely invaluable source of free 'how to' books. Create a free registration to use the site and you can then download e-books (saved in PDF format) on an enormous number of topics, including business/office subjects.

<u>www.deskdemon.com</u>   An information portal with lots of different useful sections for PAs and administrators. Launched in the UK in August 2000, DeskDemon is continually developed in close collaboration with PAs, Office Managers, secretaries and administrative staff to offer a single web site encompassing all aspects of office management.

<u>www.pa-assist.com</u>   A web portal with lots of relevant suppliers and links. Sign up for their free monthly email newsletter from 'Moneypenny' – full of useful information and reminders of special dates.

<u>www.executivesecretary.com</u>   The Executive Secretary magazine website has a huge listing of training events scheduled worldwide – click the EVENTS AND TRAINING link to reach this. All events are listed in date order, plus there is a search facility to find something near you. Equally, if you are going to put on a training event and would like to publicise it, you can do so via the site.

<u>picaaurum.tradepub.com</u>   A free-to-register website which contains over 4,000 free downloadable items, including eBooks, articles, white papers, book summaries, webinars – on an enormous array of topics for business professionals worldwide. The process to download items is a three-step process – (a) browse the catalogue of items, find an item you want and click "download", (b) go to your email inbox and open the resulting email which contains a clickable Download link – (c) then click the link which takes you to the actual

download page and downloads the item direct to your computer or device. It is a little long-winded, but the site's owners want to check that downloaders are real people, not machines stripping their databanks dry! It is well worth the effort though – in the space of a few months I've downloaded really useful CPD many items. Counting the usual Amazon price for the eBooks alone I have saved several hundred dollars / pounds.

Twitter #adminchat

#ADMINCHAT is a free session of training, advice and chat for administrative professionals worldwide, and takes place weekly on Twitter on Thursdays at 6pm UTC.

With a different guest "expert" each week, host Lucy Brazier runs a one hour Q&A session, based on the expert's chosen topic.

Admins are encouraged to read along with the chat – and join in if they wish to, by asking their own questions on the topic or offering their own responses to questions posed by others.

To be part of the experience, you first need to have a Twitter account – register for free for this.

Then you need a space where you can follow the conversation. It is conducted via tweets – so every message is 140 characters or less – and each and every one of those messages ends with the hashtag #adminchat. This is what allows users to follow the Q&A session easily, as you can search for the '#adminchat' hashtag. This is easiest done on a separate website than Twitter – for example www.twubs.com where you would sign in using your Twitter account name and password and then search for #adminchat to follow the conversation and participate.

Each question is labelled with "Q1", "Q2", etc., and answers from the guest expert are labelled "A1", "A2" etc. accordingly, with answers usually spreading over a number of tweets.

It is a great opportunity to take part in a discussion, learn something new, and meet / network with other members of the global PA / EA community.

If you aren't able to attend the one hour session, email Lucy's PA Matthew Want, wantmatthew@gmail.com, the following day to request a transcript.

www.linkedin.com

Global networking site for business professionals.

How to connect with Angela Garry on LinkedIn:

- Join the site and create your own profile page
- Search for 'Angela Garry' or go to www.linkedin.com/in/angelagarry
- Click the blue 'Connect' button
- Enter email address (angelagarry@picaaurum.com) if prompted
- Submit to send an invitation.

Whether you choose to connect with further people on the site or not, the one thing I would recommend that you definitely do is to join at least one of the growing number of discussion groups for PAs and EAs. In particular, I'd recommend you join the following discussion group:

- PAs, EAs, VAs and senior Administrators (https://www.linkedin.com/groups/PAs-EAs-VAs-Senior-Administrators-40140/about)

I created this group in 2007 and at the point of this book going to press the group has over 72,000 members worldwide. It is a great opportunity for you to network with fellow PAs and EAs globally, as well as Virtual Assistants and others working in senior admin roles – and you can post questions to seek their help and assistance.

Reading some of the existing discussions in a group will give you a good feel for how the system works – so go ahead, join a group or two, and start participating! There is so much you can learn from your peers.

Major Annual PA events – UK and Ireland

These are some of the major exhibitions / expos / trade fairs / PA programmes that are currently available within the UK and Ireland.

For the most up-to-date details on each event, check their websites for information.

There are an enormous number of events taking place all over the world each year – this list gives you just a taste of the major events on my home ground.

(Events are arranged in approximate calendar order – dates are, of course, subject to variation each year.)

February – International Confex and OMPA (Office Manager and PA Show) – London

International Confex connects event organisers with an exciting line up of venues, destinations and event support services.

For more details visit their website http://www.international-confex.com

The event includes the Office Manager and PA Show: see http://www.om-pa.co.uk

A mix of business, networking and educational opportunities.

Major event with 2,000+ PAs attending over 2 or 3 days.

February – Business Travel Show – London

Another popular annual show for those of you with responsibilities for business travel for your Executive / Manager. An excellent opportunity to make connections with a wide range of business travel specialists. http://www.businesstravelshow.com

Major event with 2,000+ PAs attending over 2 or 3 days.

March / April – ExecutiveSecretaryLIVE – London

Featuring top trainers for Assistants, handpicked for their exceptional content and delivery. See more details on their website http://executivesecretarylive.com/london .

Usual attendance: around 150 PAs from the UK, Europe and sometimes much further afield!

April / May – ExecSEC Summit – usually in Oxfordshire

Free event (including accommodation) for a group of selected PAs, enabling you to have one-to-one meetings with a range of suppliers / venues / services.

Usual attendance: around 75 PAs, and 100+ suppliers.

Programme includes some training / CPD sessions. www.forumevents.co.uk for details.

May – Zoom In's Executive PA, Secretary and Admin Forum – Dublin

Annual conference for PAs. Details via www.zoomin.ie

Attendance: around 100 PAs.

June – ACES conference for Executive Secretaries – held in Scotland.

Annual conference, in its 8th year in 2015.

Attendance: around 100 PAs.

September / October – office* – London

Annual exhibition and conference for PAs, EAs, Office Managers and VAs. Follow updates on their website http://www.officeshow.co.uk

Attendance: 4,000+ PAs over 2 days.

Resources by email

You may also like to subscribe for certain items by email:

Project management tips:

tips@projectmanager.com

Time management tips:

www.clareevans.co.uk

Email handling tips:

www.mesmo.co.uk/services/e-briefing

Sign up for the PA-Assist.com monthly newsletter:

www.pa-assist.com

You are also very welcome to use my websites for resources – details of training courses, details of useful books and magazines, links to other PA trainers and authors, useful websites and so on.

www.angelagarry.com
Main portal website, with links to all my other work: Pica Aurum, Golden Magpie, PICA BOOKS, NAHPA, UNIPA, my singing / songwriting, etc.

www.picaaurum.com
My PA training website, includes details of my forthcoming training courses worldwide.

www.goldenmagpie.co.uk
My life and career coaching and counselling website.

www.picabooks.co.uk
My publishing house for books for adults, young adults and children.

www.facebook.com/picaaurum
My Facebook Pica Aurum page.

www.nahpa.org.uk
National Association of Headteachers' PAs magazine.

Coming soon: www.unipa.org.uk
The University PAs magazine.

ANDY CASE

ABOUT THE ILLUSTRATOR

ANDY CASE

The multi-talented ANDY CASE created the illustrations included in this book, based on discussions with the author.

Andy writes:

"I've been a professional cartoonist and illustrator since the age of 13. Illustration has always been a passion for me and I hope it continues to do so.

The most satisfying aspect of creating an illustration or cartoon, is seeing it come to life and recognising that it has a personality and this influences everything it does. In the 22 years I've been a professional cartoonist, I've never lost sight of this. This has helped my passion grow and my style mature. During my career, I have been lucky enough to have produce illustrations for books, magazines, galleries, and a myriad of organisations."

Contact details: andycasestudios@gmail.com

Website: andycasestudios.weebly.com

ANGELA GARRY

ABOUT THE AUTHOR

ANGELA GARRY

With over 22,000 first-level contacts on business networking site LinkedIn – and a three-level network extending to more than 38 million – Angela Garry is the most connected person in the world with the job titles of 'personal assistant' and 'PA trainer'.

Angela qualified as a Secondary School Mathematics teacher in 1991 with a BSc(Ed) and QTS from the University of Exeter.

Since then she has worked in administrative roles in England and Ireland, with 18 years of this in Personal Assistant roles. She has worked in two global banks, three universities, a sixth-form college, a water and sewerage utility, an engineering consultancy, an international seaport, a government-sponsored employment training company and an executive search company, plus her most recent role for over five years as the principal's PA at a brand new academy for 11–19 year olds in Nottingham, England.

Angela received her PostGraduate Certificate in Integrative Psychotherapy from the University of Coventry in 2013.

Having been shortlisted for both the UK Headteachers' PA of the Year and The Times/Hays PA of the Year awards in 2011, Angela has combined her teaching and PA skills to quickly become a renowned trainer, and is now a leading expert in educational administration training.

She has delivered highly successful training and networking events and seminars for PAs since 2010 around the world – including the UK and Ireland, Norway, Switzerland, Russia, United Arab Emirates, Kenya, Tanzania, South Africa, Singapore, Thailand, Hong Kong and China – offering training courses to a variety of audiences from both corporate / industry and educational institutions.

Since 2012, she has also been a leading educational administration trainer, creating and delivering training programmes specifically designed for educational PAs, and has worked with more than 350 executives' PAs and administrative staff from over 250 international schools and independent schools worldwide.

In total, Angela has trained, coached, mentored, presented to and worked with more than 3,000 PAs, EAs, secretaries and administrators to date.

In April 2012, Angela created her training company, Pica Aurum, with the aim of helping everybody find and reach their potential. Through Pica Aurum she offers training and mentoring worldwide, together with career coaching, life coaching, counselling and psychotherapy in her local area.

During her role in a new school, Angela was interviewed by NAHPA, the National Association of Headteachers' PAs magazine, in 2010. Writing subsequent articles resulted in her being invited to take over as the magazine's Editor in 2012 – and, when the publishers decided to close the magazine, she took over its ownership in April 2015. The magazine is the UK's leading publication for PAs and administrators working in schools – and she is looking to launch a sister magazine for University PAs in 2016.

In addition, Angela has been a regular contributor since 2009 to several other leading PA magazines, including Executive Secretary, PA Enterprise, PA Life and Executive PA.

Angela Garry is currently available for bookings worldwide – as a trainer, motivational speaker, conference chair, for book signings and readings, and as a mentor or coach.

Her first book "Brave PAs", for assistants working in education, was published in Spring 2015.

"The PA / EA Circus" is her second book for assistants, this time in a corporate / industry setting.

Being a PA for many years, Angela is well used to multi-tasking – and is now concentrating on continuing to build her training business, publishing NAHPA magazine and launching the new UNIPA sister magazine, as well as her new venture in writing books for children and young adults.

For more information, resources, dates of courses, subscriptions to NAHPA magazine, etc., please visit:

www.angelagarry.com – portal linking to all her websites.

To contact Angela directly: email angelagarry@picaaurum.com

Made in the USA
Charleston, SC
27 September 2015